Teach your child to

Sleep

Teach your child to

Sleep

Gentle sleep solutions
for babies and children

hamlyn

An Hachette UK Company

www.hachette.co.uk

First published in Great Britain in 2005 by Hamlyn, an imprint of
Octopus Publishing Group Ltd
Carmelite House
50 Victoria Embankment
London EC4Y 0DZ
www.octopusbooks.co.uk
www.octopusbooksusa.com

This edition published in 2020

Copyright © Octopus Publishing Group Ltd 2005, 2016, 2020

Distributed in the US by Hachette Book Group
1290 Avenue of the Americas , 4th and 5th Floors
New York, NY 10104

Distributed in Canada by Canadian Manda Group
664 Annette St., Toronto, Ontario, Canada M6S 2C8

ISBN 9780600636533

A CIP catalogue record for this book is available from the British Library.

Printed and bound in China

10 9 8 7 6 5 4 3 2 1

Group Publishing Director: Denise Bates
Assistant Editor: Emily Brickell
Copy Editor: Jemima Dunne
Senior Designer: Jaz Bahra
Design: Geoff Fennell and Jeremy Tilston
Senior Production Controller: Allison Gonsalves

Contents

Millpond Children's Sleep Clinic's approach

There is one topic that probably preoccupies the conversations of parents of babies and young children more than any other – sleep, and how to get more of it.

Is he/she a good sleeper? is often the first question parents are asked. The monopoly sleep has on parents' conversations is not surprising – research shows roughly 30 per cent of parents report their infant or child to have sleep problems.

Helping a child to sleep well can appear complex in nature as often sleep issues have been long lasting and multi-faceted. Luckily, once you have isolated the nature of the problem there is a choice of solutions with which to resolve them.

The strategies we use at Millpond are well-recognized, fully-researched, evidence-based techniques used by professionals worldwide. What distinguishes our approach is that we do not adhere to any one technique in a given situation. We believe that the solution to any family's sleep issue must take into account their environment, composition, needs and expectations, their child's personality and temperament, medical conditions, diet and developmental stage. We believe in a tailor-made approach, sympathetic rather than prescriptive, and always has your child at its centre.

All the solutions recommended in this book are used at Millpond. They have worked for many thousands of children – and their exhausted parents – and we hope that, through this book, they will work for many more.

Although we have over 20 years experience with children's sleep problems, we are not just health professionals with an academic knowledge of sleep disorders. All of our sleep consultants are mothers who have been through it with their own children. We know how tough it can be to deal with and that, with support and clear direction, you can help your child to sleep well.

While we are confident that our methods can help resolve babies' and children's sleep issues, every child is different. Only you really know what your child is ready for or capable of. We aim to guide you through the options so you can choose the right solution for you and your child. Our experience tells us that you are only a few weeks away from having a baby or child who knows how to sleep well, enjoys going to bed and wakes happily in the morning. We hope that on the way you will have learnt enough to manage any other sleep dilemmas that may occur in the future.

The name of our clinic was chosen to reflect the transition from chaos to calm that comes with teaching your child to sleep well. We hope that, with the help of this book, we can help you make that transition.

Mandy Gurney

How to use this book

This book is designed to help you to understand the nature of the sleep issue that you and your child are experiencing, and to identify an appropriate solution. Knowing exactly why, when and how your child should sleep, and sharing in the experiences of other parents, will help you move towards practical solutions.

You can use this book in a number of ways. Reading chapter by chapter will give you an overall view of basic sleep patterns and needs, followed by practical solutions for dealing with problems. If you wish to tackle specific areas you can turn to the practical chapters first and read the theory later.

Chapter-by-chapter approach
The book describes what sleep is all about and how it develops as a child grows.

Chapter 1 Examines the basics of sleep, such as why children need sleep, what makes them sleepy, how sleep patterns change and how normal development influences their sleep. A little knowledge of the science of sleep will give you a head start in improving your child's sleep.

Chapter 2 Looks at how good sleep habits are formed, and how you can adapt your circumstances to encourage good habits.

Chapter 3 Looks at the types and causes of the wide range of sleep issues we deal with as clinicians at Millpond Children's Sleep Clinic.

Chapter 4 Describes the various solutions that can be applied to improve your child's sleep. This will guide you onto the right path for your child.

Chapter 5 A series of flow charts designed to help you identify the nature of your child's sleep issue and directs you to more detailed supporting information elsewhere in the book.

Chapter 6 Describes the programmes put in place by the families we have advised over the past 20 years. The experiences of these families are both instructive and encouraging; you will see how the principles outlined earlier in the book have been successfully applied.

Key sleep issues
Many parents will have bought this book because they are experiencing specific sleep issues with their child and wish to find a solution. If this is the case, turning to specific practical sections of this book will help to show that no problem is insurmountable, and that there are simple steps that you can take to overcome them.

Please recognize though that the advice contained in this book is for otherwise healthy children. If your child has an underlying medical condition, you will almost certainly need to address this first. Similarly, if your child is currently unwell, wait until he is fully recovered before using these techniques and plans.

Turn to **Chapter 3**, pages 50–65, for common sleep problems.

If you want to know if you are encouraging good sleep habits, turn to **Dos and don'ts** on pages 48–49.

If you believe you know the cause of your child's sleep problem, but need help in assessing your situation, see **Ten key questions** on pages 68–69.

Turn to pages 112–155 for **Sleep solutions**.

If you are experiencing problems applying your sleep plan, look at **What if...?** pages 84–89.

Turn to **Chapter 5**, pages 90–111, to find flow charts that will help you to tailor a strategy to suit your particular family situation.

If you want to read about real-life situations, and how they were overcome, read through the case studies in **Chapter 6**, pages 112–155.

Identifying your priorities

How and why do you want to help your child to sleep? This may seem an odd question, but parents have different goals and motives for their children's sleep, and different hopes for the outcome.

Some parents may want their baby to sleep through the night as soon as possible, especially if all of their friend's babies already seem to be doing so. Others are happy to let time be their guide, ignoring social and media pressure, allowing their baby's spontaneous and natural sleep patterns to set the agenda.

Before you decide on your course of action, take some time to decide where you are on this spectrum and talk to your partner about it. It will enable you both to be realistic about what is possible, what is practical for you and your family and to establish your ideals and expectations.

Realistic goals are easier to meet and less stressful on you as parents. You are more likely to achieve them if you start when you feel ready, work at your own pace and feel in control. If you are currently unsure quite what your hopes and expectations are, or if you are even ready to make any changes at all, answering the questions in the box below should help you.

What is your parenting style?

There are a range of strategies and solutions for dealing with your child's sleep (see chapter 4, pages 66–89). It is important before you start to

Questions to ask yourself

Before you consider starting on a sleep plan, consider the following questions:

• Does my child really have a sleep problem? If you are unsure, see What to expect of your child's sleep see pages 14–15.

• What are my goals for my child's sleep, and are they realistic for his age?

• Could a medical condition or pain be impacting on my child's sleep?

• Do my partner and I both agree something needs to be done and can we be consistent and support each other?

• Is this practically and emotionally the right time to start a sleep programme?

• If I am struggling and need support can I ask family or friends for help?

For a more detailed exploration, see Ten key questions – assessing your child's sleep, pages 68–69.

**What are my goals for
my child's sleep?**

address any that you take time to consider what would suit your parenting style, your goals and your expectations. Naturally your child is your main focus and his needs are at the heart of this, but it is also important to consider your own attitudes to life – and your own limitations.

The sleep programme that you choose is more likely to work if it has some compatibility with your parenting style. This also applies to ensuring agreement between you and your partner, as a sleep problem shared is a sleep problem partly solved. Whether one or both of you are on the case, and whether or not you have similar parenting styles, consistency is the golden rule to work at together at all times.

Look from your child's point of view

When examining the different strategies open to you, it is even more important to consider what is right for your child. Research has shown strong links with a child's personality and temperament and their sleep. Considering whether your child is particularly determined, very resistant or sensitive to change, or fearful or anxious at bedtime or in the night, will help you decide what you should do and how. It will also set up

expectations for how your baby or child might respond to your changes.

If you are dealing with the sleep concerns of your second or subsequent child, he may not be like his older brother or sister, so it is highly likely that the same strategy will not work for both and you will need to adjust and adopt different strategies for this child.

And lastly, if you have identified a solution or experienced an effective method in the past, remember that children change. What worked when your child was 12 months old is unlikely to work in the same way if sleep problems recur when he is three years old.

Child-carers can help

If your baby or child is being cared for by someone else during the day, you will need to involve them in your plans. Make sure they fully understand how important it is for your child that everyone follows your plan and remains consistent. Write it out for them to follow so there is no confusion. If you are filling in a sleep diary, ask them to complete the times when they are looking after your child.

Understanding sleep

The importance of sleep

We now know, thanks to extensive scientific investigation, what happens to our brains and bodies during different stages of sleep. However, there are still some unanswered questions, and strangely one of those is why we need sleep in the first place.

Sleep is a vital function that affects our physical and mental functioning profoundly. We spend about a third of our lives asleep and we cannot do without it. We know that a good night's sleep leaves us refreshed, alert and confident to face the challenges of the day. Conversely, a bad night's sleep deprives us of the concentration, energy and ability to do the things we need to in everyday life. We become more irritable, moody and negative, and are more likely to fall out with loved ones. Not only does our memory suffer, but we are more likely to pile on the pounds as we head for the biscuits for that hit of sugar.

But the effect on babies and children is even more profound (see below and opposite). Insufficient sleep compromises their ability to learn, stay fit and healthy, and even grow. Conversely, studies have shown that learning to sleep better lifts children's mood and enhances their intellectual ability.

How lack of sleep affects children

Anyone who has a baby or child who hasn't slept well is familiar with the result. Babies can be restless, fractious and difficult to settle or calm, getting into a pattern of snack feeding and snack sleeping; falling asleep part way through a feed, only to wake up 30 minutes later still hungry, often in a tired, restless state. In toddlers it often leads to impatience, poor appetite, clinginess and temperamental behaviour. And it can 'snowball' as, paradoxically, the overtired baby or child finds it more difficult to sleep.

Sleep studies have shown how lack of sleep can affect a child's learning, academic potential, concentration and ability to focus. A sleep-deprived child finds it much harder to regulate their emotions and parents often find their behaviour more challenging. Pre-school children in particular are more at risk of accidents when tired. Scientists now believe lack of sleep to be one of the main contributing factors in the obesity epidemic; the less a child sleeps the less likely they are to exercise and more likely they are eat high-calorie foods.

The good news is that by learning to sleep well, these affects can be reversed and a child's behaviour and performance can improve dramatically and quickly. Their mood is often demonstrably elevated, making them easier to care for at every age, both inside and outside the home. School teachers have reported that

Why young brains need sleep

When a baby or child sleeps the brain is very active.

- The brain consolidates new memories and connects new experiences with old memories to help children make sense of their world.

- The brain's ability for learning is restored by making way for new memories.

- The body lays down muscle memories.

- Sleep helps with focus, learning and concentration.

- Creativity, problem-solving and decision-making are enhanced.

Why young bodies need sleep

When children sleep, the body restores itself and essential processes take place.

- Vital hormones are released to help growth and repair.
- White blood cells are produced, supporting the immune system and fighting infection.
- The hormones grehlin and leptin, which control our appetite and satiety, are re-balanced, keeping body weight in check.
- Blood is directed to developing muscles.

children who have more sleep show improved concentration and application in the classroom and are more likely to enjoy their nursery or school environment.

Your sleep matters too

The effect of sleep deprivation is not just restricted to your children. The irregular sleep patterns of a child who has not yet learnt to sleep predictably also deprive their parents of the sleep they too need. Being on call, especially during the night, for restless children can leave you feeling like you have interminable jet-lag, without the

holiday photographs for comfort. Research backs up the impact lack of sleep can have on the whole family and how relationships and parent's mental health can suffer.

It may be the effect that the lack of sleep is having on the whole family is one of your reasons for wanting to help your child sleep better. Don't dismiss this as selfish; if you are more rested, you will feel better equipped both emotionally and physically to handle your baby, toddler or child. Your confidence as a parent will increase, and a more confident parent results in a happier child. We have found that the effect can go much further. When a baby's or child's sleep problem is solved, the spirit of the whole family lifts.

Sleeping for life

A child who learns to sleep well in her early years not only reaps the immediate psychological and physical rewards, she also learns good habits that will benefit her for life. Studies have shown that young children whose sleep issues go unaddressed are more susceptible to sleep problems into adulthood.

Teaching children to sleep well at a young age does not just benefit the parents who are caring for them; it also sets up habits that will help sustain them through the changing challenges and pressures of their teenage and adult years, when the energy and clarity of a rested mind and body will give them the resources they need.

Good sleep is essential for your child's physical and emotional wellbeing.

What to expect of your child's sleep

As with any other aspect of your child's daily life and development, you just get used to one new stage and then another one comes along. Sleep is no different, but having an understanding of how it develops will help you know what to expect, to have realistic goals and to be prepared for any upcoming changes.

Young babies have completely different sleep phases and schedules to us, and generally unpredictable sleep habits. As they mature so their sleep alters in terms of how much they need and how it is structured over a 24-hour period (see below). Being aware of this difference, helps you know what to expect, and when you might need to help out if you have concerns.

Average sleep needs in childhood

Understanding the average amount of sleep your child needs for their age will give you a good point to work towards. Bear in mind that your child may need a little more or less sleep than average, but that any variation should not be too far off. This table is a guide showing average amounts of sleep for both day and night – the hours of sleep for infants and older babies is not continuous. Over childhood sleep slowly declines to reach an average of nine hours per night for the average teenager.

Age	Average number of hours of sleep needed		Total sleep over 24-hours
	Daytime	Night-time	
1 week	8	8.5	16.5
4 weeks	6–8	8–9	14–17
3 months	5–6	9–11	14–17
4 months	3–4	9–11	12–15
6 months	3–4	10–11	13–15
9 months	2–3	10–12	12–15
12 months	2–3	10–11	12–14
2 years	1.5–2	10–12	11.5–14
3 years	0–1	10–13	10–14
4 to 6 years	–	10-13	10-13

Figures taken from the National Sleep Foundation (2015)

Birth to four months

In the early weeks babies sleep for an average of 16 hours out of every 24, equally divided between day and night. Life for you would be very simple if this came in one big chunk, but of course it is split into many periods of two to four hours scattered throughout your own sleeping and waking times.

This unpredictable pattern happens because the biological clock, or circadian rhythm, is slow to develop, so new babies cannot distinguish night from day. Instead they rely on their tummies, and wake and sleep depending on whether they feel hungry or sated. In the first eight weeks, your newborn is likely to be awake for about two hours, then sleep for anything from 30 minutes to three hours at a time.

By the age of eight to ten weeks most babies can distinguish night from day, a stage of development that parents greet with great relief. And as their daytime naps drop from about four to three by the end of the third month, they start to sleep for longer periods at night too.

Young babies sleep also looks very different from ours in their first six months; they do not experience the different stages of sleep as adults do. Instead they experience active sleep (our rapid-eye movement, REM, sleep), and quiet sleep (our non-rapid-eye-movement, NREM, sleep).

See also Sleep cycles, pages 16–17.

Four to six months

As sleep consolidation continues, babies now sleep for longer stretches at night. The hormone melatonin is now influencing their maturing sleep patterns and they enter into deep sleep at the start of the night.

Your baby's naps will probably start about two hours after last waking in the morning. As he becomes skilled at recognizing cues from you and is able to understand what is happening this is the perfect time to introduce a bedtime routine, if you haven't done so already.

Six months to one year

There is now a distinct shift in the balance of night-time and daytime sleep. Six- to eight-month-old babies usually still need three naps a day, but, by nine months most need just one morning and one afternoon nap.

By the age of six months your baby's sleeping and waking patterns are more organized so he is able to sleep for longer at night. However, research shows night waking is still very common, and babies only predictably sleep all night, every night at close to one year old. But as naps and night-time sleep become more predictable, you can plan activities around your baby and, importantly, to get more regular, unbroken sleep yourselves.

One to three years

At some point over the middle of this period, most toddlers will shift their morning nap to around lunchtime and sleep for one and half to two hours, which means that they can drop their afternoon nap.

Towards the age of three, the length of your child's nap may decrease to about 45 minutes and he will sleep for 10–13 hours at night. Good sleeping habits can easily be disrupted by a holiday, illness, or a change in sleeping arrangements now as the circadian rhythm is still developing and is easily upset. So, it is important to maintain your regular bedtime routine and waking time.

Three to six years

By the middle of this period, circadian rhythms are fully established and between the age of three and four years children drop daytime naps. However, they still need an average of 10–13 hours sleep a night; a shortage of sleep is likely to have an impact on their behaviour and learning.

Sleep cycles

Sleep is not a single state and is not, as was commonly thought, simply the opposite of 'awake'. A normal night's sleep is made up of several identifiable cycles, which we can consciously distinguish, and have different biological functions.

This applies to people of any age, but the cycles occur in different quantities and at different times in babies and young children. Knowing when and why they occur can help you understand your child's sleep patterns, which in turn helps you to determine whether they are indicative of a sleep issue or simply a reflection of these natural cycles.

Types of sleep

Scientists categorize sleep into two main stages: rapid eye movement (REM) sleep, and deeper, non-rapid-eye-movement (NREM) sleep, which has three different stages, see below. Overnight, the brain cycles repeatedly through REM and non-REM sleep approximately every 90 minutes, passing from drowsiness down through light and dream sleep into increasingly deeper sleep.

In babies under the age of six months, sleep stages are very different: REM sleep is known as active sleep and NREM sleep is known as quiet sleep.

Rapid eye movement (REM) sleep

In this sleep state a person's eyes can be seen moving rapidly under closed eyelids. We dream during REM sleep and, to prevent us acting out our dreams, we are in a semi-paralysed state. It is the first sleep state to develop – babies experience it in the womb at about six months' gestation – and it is vital to brain development. During this part of the sleep cycle, the body switches off and the brain receives extra blood and warms up, indicating a greater level of activity. REM sleep helps us processes what we have seen and done during our waking hours to make sense of our world, process emotional memories and make connections with things we already know.

Because of its developmental importance, babies spend a lot of time in REM sleep. An unborn baby spends almost all of its time in a sleep-like state, much of which resembles REM sleep. REM-like sleep accounts for 50 per cent of a newborn's sleep state. By the age of three years only around 33 per cent is REM sleep and in later childhood and into adulthood, it makes up 25 per cent.

Parents of toddlers will have noticed that, from the age of about two, most children are aware of their dreams, which can be very vivid, and start to talk about them. You can see it in action for yourself. Most children twitch occasionally in their sleep, move their eyeballs back and forth under their eyelids, and breathe irregularly when they dream.

The proportion of REM sleep increases as the night progresses, and is at its greatest in the early hours of the morning. This sleep state is mentally restorative, which is why a person (adult or child) who is woken up too early often feels mentally 'foggy' for the rest of the day. (see Your sleep matters too – look after yourself, page 65).

Non-rapid-eye-movement (NREM) sleep

This is a state of slow-wave sleep, during which blood is released to the muscles, tissue is grown or repaired, and hormones are released for growth and development. Your child will lie quietly, her muscles will be relaxed, and her breathing will be deep and steady, and she will not move. This is the state most people think of as true sleep and it accounts for about 75 per cent of total time spent in sleep.

There are 3 stages identified in NREM sleep:

Stage 1 Known as sleep latency, or dropping off to sleep, this stage lasts up to five minutes.

Stage 2 This is the beginning of true sleep and lasts ten to 25 minutes. Our muscles relax, heart rate slows, and we have a loss of conscious awareness.

Sleep stages in the older baby

From approximately four months babies start their night with a period of deep NREM sleep. Throughout the night they cycle several times through all stages of REM and NREM sleep.

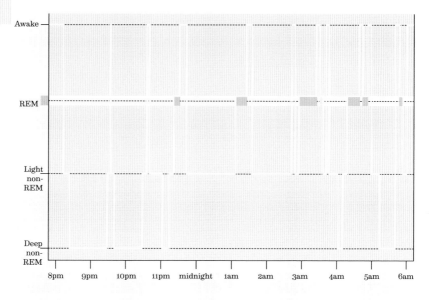

Stage 3 This is very deep slow-wave restorative sleep. Breathing and heart rate are slow and regular, and the muscles relax. It is very hard to wake a person from this sleep state and if you do, they are often disorientated and take a while to come round. This state is thought to be very important for growth and development.

What sleep cycles mean for your child

Each sleep cycle in a full-term newborn is about 50–60 minutes long, but by the age of three to four months it starts to increase to about 90 minutes, a pattern that is maintained for life. However long the cycle, it is in the lighter moments of sleep between cycles that your child is most likely to rouse. You may see her stir at this point, often moving or muttering – but if she's left undisturbed she may go back to sleep.

A newborn will enter the REM-like sleep state as soon as she falls asleep, while an older baby or child will go into NREM sleep first. It generally takes about 15 minutes for your baby to fall asleep

fully, although most children do so more quickly. Once asleep, it takes about 10 minutes to enter deep sleep; waking your child from this deep state of sleep may be almost impossible. This is very relevant when applying a sleep strategy (see pages 72–81). Taking a long time to go to sleep may be indicative of: a stimulating bedtime routine, irregular sleep/wake patterns, anxiety, late naps (see pages 32–35) or inappropriate sleep-onset associations (see page 53).

Unfortunately, adult sleep cycles do not coincide with those of children, so your child may rouse when you are in the depths of your deep sleep or wake you early in the morning when you are having your very important REM sleep. There is little you can do about this, except share the visits to your child with your partner.

What makes us sleepy?

Sleep is regulated by two distinct and separate body systems: homeostasis, or the sleep drive, and the circadian rhythm, or body clock. The two systems work closely together to regulate when we are sleepy and when we are awake.

Homeostasis

In essence sleep/wake homeostasis creates a drive that balances sleep and wakefulness. Our sleep drive becomes stronger every hour we are awake, then causes us to sleep longer and more deeply after a period of sleep deprivation. Production of the body chemical, adenosine, increases with each hour of wakefulness, creating a desire and a need to sleep – the longer we are awake the greater the pressure is.

The sleep drive can be inhibited, or reduced, by a number of factors including the stimulant caffeine, which blocks adenosine receptors. Caffeine has a half-life of five to seven hours, so the cup of coffee, tea or high caffeine drink you had at 4.00pm to help keep you going, could still be impacting on your sleep at 10.30pm. Other factors that influence adenosine levels include napping too close to bedtime and stress.

As we sleep our adenosine level dramatically decreases, removing the pressure to sleep. This goes some way to explain why when your child wakes in the early hours of the morning it is much harder for him to go back to sleep.

Homeostasis also plays an important role helping us maintain sleep throughout the night. It ensures we have enough sleep to make up for the hours we spend awake in the day.

Circadian rhythm

This is the system that regulates a range of daily functions such as body temperature, hormone release, and metabolism. It also regulates our feelings of sleepiness and wakefulness over a 24-hour period. Circadian rhythm, or body clock, is governed by a complex group of neurons in our brain called the suprachiasmatic nucleus (SCN) – the master body clock.

The body clock naturally rises in the morning enabling us to be awake and alert, ready to start the day, and continues to do so all morning, promoting wakefulness, reaching a peak around midday. From then it starts to fall; our biggest dips occur between 1pm and 3pm and between 2am and 4am. These times can vary if you are a night owl or a lark (see right) and the dip will be deeper and more pronounced if you are sleep deprived.

As the day progresses, your circadian rhythm continues to fall, and you become less alert. By bedtime, the pressure to sleep is very high, while the alerting effect of our body clock is low, which creates the optimal opportunity to sleep. The circadian rhythm drops to the lowest level as you sleep, helping to promote and maintain sleep.

How light and dark effects our body clock

Our body clock responds to light and dark signals, which come via the optic nerve at the back of the eye. In the morning, light travels to the master clock signalling that it is time to wake. It sends messages to other parts of our brain to raise our body temperature and release hormones such as cortisol, needed to wake us. In the evening, lower light levels signal the master clock to release the sleep hormone melatonin into the blood stream via the pineal gland.

Receiving bright light at the 'wrong' time of the day (such as light from a hand-held device or screen at bedtime) can confuse the body clock, upsetting its rhythm; this can impact on health, energy levels, mood and sleep.

What is your chronotype?

Chronotype describes the time of day when you feel most alert or energetic – whether you are a morning lark or a night owl, or somewhere between the two. If you prefer to go to bed early and wake early, you are a 'morning type' or 'lark'. Or if a later bedtime and wake-up time suits you better, you are an 'evening type', or 'owl'.

Your chronotype is inherited from your parents, genetically determined in the same way as your eye colour. Your natural sleep rhythm is passed on to you through the PER3 gene.

Larks make up roughly 40 per cent and owls 30 per cent of the population with the remainder coming somewhere in between. Knowing your chronotype will help you sleep better, and plan your day knowing when you perform at your best. Larks tend to function well in the mornings, when owls are slowly coming round. Whereas owls come into their own late in the day and evening times, when larks are ready to put their feet up.

As well as knowing how much sleep your child needs (see pages 14–15), identifying his chronotype means you will be able to establish a sleep pattern for him in line with his natural body clock. Work out which chronotype best describes you and your partner and use this as a basis for your child's bedtime and waking time. By working with his natural body clock this way he will fall asleep faster, have better-quality and the right amount of sleep and wake less at night.

Larks A lark child is likely to need an earlier bedtime. Putting your lark to bed later usually means he will have less sleep that night, as he is still likely to wake at his typically early time.

Owls An owl child is likely to have a slightly later bed and wake-up times than his lark-like friend. It is particularly important for him to have a regular set bedtime and, just as importantly, a fixed wake-up time. If put to bed late, he is likely to wake later too. If this pattern is repeated, for example over school holidays, his body clock will shift into a later phase. Limiting light exposure in the evening and having a good dose of light in the morning will help keep an owl child's body clock on track.

Dim light in the evening helps with melatonin production.

Developmental stages and sleep

If the pattern of your child's life didn't change from one week to the next and it was all very predictable, it would be easy. But, of course, babies and children develop differently and do things at their own pace. Sometimes changes interfere with the process of sleep (often referred to as 'sleep regression'); other developments help your child's sleep. Anticipating these changes, and their impact, can make it easier to adapt to them.

Birth to six months

It is our internal 24-hour body clock, or circadian rhythm, which tells us when to sleep, when to wake and when to eat. Our brain uses light in the day to reset its body clock and at night it is darkness that helps our body know it's time for sleep (see page 18).

In the dark environment of the womb babies do not have light to help signal the difference between night and day. Research has shown for the majority of pregnancy the baby will be asleep. It is not until your last trimester that your baby will spend brief periods of two or three hours per day awake. Before birth it is your movement and your melatonin, which the baby receives via the placenta, that helps to regulate your unborn baby's sleep. Your newborn must develop both her own body clock and start her own hormone production. This takes place during the first three months, and until then her nights and days will simply blend together.

Your newborn baby will spend on average 16 hours a day sleeping with her sleep split roughly 50:50 between the day and night in short sleep cycles. Babies' sleep is governed by their tiny tummies and their need to feed and so their sleep episodes will be brief, and they wake every two to three hours for milk.

By ten weeks most babies will have developed the ability to tell the difference between day and night, and by three months they will be sleeping longer at night than the day. Furthermore, many will have the ability to sleep in longer chunks at night of perhaps five or six hours.

By the age of three months your baby will be increasingly stimulated by her surroundings and will be becoming skilled at recognizing cues from her parents. As she now understands what is happening, it is the perfect time to introduce a bedtime routine and cues for sleep, if you haven't done so already. As her sleep patterns are maturing, she will enter into deep sleep at the start of the night (see pages 16–17).

Her night-time sleep cycles slowly start to extend to 90 minutes and daytime sleep cycles start to increase to 45 minutes, a pattern that is set for the rest of her life. This means she will rouse less often during sleep and sleep for longer periods. By now she will probably be sleeping about twice as long at night as in the day.

By 10 weeks most babies can distinguish between night and day.

Develop-
mental
milestones/
stages
that may
affect sleep
birth to six
months

NEWBORN BABY

- Cannot tell the difference between night and day.

- Has mainly REM-like, active, or light, sleep and very little quiet, or deep, sleep.

- Has short sleep cycles – 60 minutes at night and 30 minutes in the day.

- Stays awake for short periods at a time – one to two hours.

- Sleeping and waking is strongly influenced by feeding.

ONE TO THREE MONTHS

- **First month** Will be able to use a range of cries so that you can begin to distinguish the difference between cries of hunger, boredom or tiredness.

- **Second month** Will be comforted by music and background sounds such as a washing machine or fan.

- **Third month** Will be able to stay awake slightly longer in the day, and by three months daytime naps are taken every two hours.

THREE TO SIX MONTHS

- Is becoming much more social and is increasingly stimulated by her surroundings.

- Can recognize cues and so, if you haven't done so yet, now is the perfect time to introduce a bedtime routine.

- Night-time sleep cycles begin to extend to 90 minutes and daytime sleep cycles to 45 minutes.

- Rouses less often in sleep and sleeps for longer periods.

- Sleep patterns are maturing so baby enters deep sleep at the start of the night.

- After six months needs daytime naps roughly every two and half hours.

- Is becoming interested by the world, so very easily distracted and over stimulated. Will settle much easier with a napping routine with quiet time before sleep.

- Towards the end of this period, darken the room for naps too.

- Colicky symptoms subside so your baby is more settled in the evening.

- Starts to roll over without help and pulls herself around the cot, so often finds herself in awkward positions in her cot.

Six months to one year

By the age of six months, your baby's sleeping and waking patterns are more organized so he can now sleep for longer periods of the night. By the time he is around eight months old his daytime naps become more predictable in both length and their timing. However, research shows night waking is still very common in this age group; babies only predictably sleep all night, every night at close to a year old.

Although most babies have settled into a bedtime routine by now, this can all too readily be disrupted by certain developmental changes.

Separation anxiety This normal stage of development starts when your baby is seven to nine months old, and can reach a peak at about 18 months old. Up until now your baby will play happily when you leave the room in the day and is content at bedtime after you have kissed him goodnight and are out of sight. But all of a sudden he starts to cry, becoming distressed and upset even if you leave the room for a matter of seconds. He has reached a stage where he knows when a person is leaving but his lack of experience means he cannot be sure that they will always come back. This anxiety can make bedtimes and nap times difficult for you both.

Having an understanding of separation anxiety can help you feel less stressed by it. You can help your baby understand you will return by playing games with him in the day. Try for example, playing peek-a-boo with a book or cloth, hide and seek in the same room, and reading lift-the-flap books together. Or try leaving the room for a second, quickly returning and giving him a kiss and gradually extending the time you are away.

Overtired or excited Make sure your baby is napping well so he is not overtired at bedtime. Try re-visiting your bedtime routine to ensure it is winding down and calm (see Creating a sleep routine pages 30–31) and if planning a sleep programme to help him settle at bedtime, it is best to choose a gentle gradual withdrawal technique with a series of small steps that he can adapt to without getting upset (see Sleep strategies, pages 72–81).

Teething Somewhere around the age of six months, your baby will start teething. Although babies vary in the amount of pain they experience it can often be the cause of discomfort at night and result in night-time waking. However, if your baby sleeps well he is likely to find teething pains less bothersome (see Teething, page 46).

Mobility Babies also become much more mobile between six and nine months, first sitting, then crawling and finally, standing. If your baby moves around when he partially wakes at night, he may be disturbed and wake up if he finds himself 'stuck' in his cot in an odd position. Research shows the onset of a new motor skill, such as crawling, can also lead to night-time sleep disruptions.

By the end of this period your baby will probably be able to stand up, often excitedly using his cot as a wonderful place to practise this incredible new skill (see What if... my baby stands up in the cot, page 84).

At around eight months old daytime sleep becomes more predictable.

Developmental milestones/ stages that may affect sleep six to 12 months

SIX TO NINE MONTHS

- Start eating solids (at six months).

- Learn to roll from back to front and vice versa.

- Start to sit unaided.

- Begin to crawl.

- Pull himself up to stand – often wanting to practice in his cot.

- Begin to understand simple instructions.

- Understand that objects exist even if they are hidden.

- Develop separation anxiety and may suddenly cry when you leave the bedroom.

- Start teething. Although pain levels can vary, almost all babies sleep will be disturbed at some point during this time.

- Your baby will have the majority of his sleep at night.

- By six months your baby will be having three distinct naps.

- By nine months your baby will drop his afternoon nap.

- Gradually stay awake happily for longer periods in the day.

NINE MONTHS TO ONE YEAR

During this period your baby may be able to:

- Listen to and follow basic actions and instructions.

- Show temper when not wanting to cooperate.

- Say his first words.

- Pull up to stand and cruise – often wanting to practice in his cot.

- Begin to walk.

By the time your child attends school, she'll no longer need a daytime nap.

One to six years

Your baby's rapid maturation into a child makes this a fascinating period. Huge leaps in progress occur that are very rewarding for parents.

Naturally, there are changes that can benefit sleep, but there are also some that can impact on sleep, although this is usually temporary. The ability of a one-year-old to walk, for example, can confer an independence that might not always be welcome at night. For example, she may find it great fun to run away from you when you want to put her to bed, or even try to climb out of her cot.

Sleep disturbances, such as nightmares and sleep talking, start to become apparent from about the age of about two years and peak when a child is around four years old. But they are also something most children grow out of (see Sleep disorders and parasomnias, pages 54–57).

Your child's increasing independence during this period can also be expressed in a resistance to bedtime. She may try to keep herself awake, even when you know she is very tired. This becomes more challenging to deal with in the second year, when she begins to talk and expresses her personality, requesting extra stories and drinks and testing your bedtime boundaries.

Around the age of two and a half many children come out of nappies during the day. Typically, most children are not dry at night until they reach the age of three and a half years, and it is not uncommon for parents to delay removing the night nappies until much later, when they feel their child is physically ready. However you approach this bear in mind that it is a rare child that never wets the bed (see Bed-wetting, pages 62–63).

By the age of three years most children are beginning to forgo their daytime nap, and many are spending tiring hours at nursery, both of which should help promote a good night's sleep. However, going to nursery or school is a big step for most children and can be one that triggers fears of separation and anxiety, which often surface at bedtime.

The rapid development in your child's powers of imagination at this age often leads to fear of the dark and nightmares, with accompanying images of monsters exacerbating the anxiety. It is best to reassure your child that these fears are common and unfounded without resorting to looking for that monster under the bed or behind the curtains (see Nightmares and night terrors, pages 55–57).

From around the age of three, children are starting to understand the correlation between their actions and receiving a reward, or the connection between their behaviour and your praise. This ability and the fact that they have learned to wait short periods for things, means this is the age at which you can implement simple reward systems to encourage and motivate them to make change (see Positive reinforcement – rewards, pages 82–83).

Developmental milestones/ stages that may affect sleep one to six years

Your child's increasing independence, her imagination and the separation starting nursery or school brings, can all interfere with her established bedtime routine. Conversely, the regulation to your child's body clock that day care and school schedules bring will help her sleep well.

ONE YEAR TO 18 MONTHS

- Will drop to one nap a day, consolidating all her daytime sleep into one longer period generally after lunch.

- May develop minor fears, for example, of animals and loud noises.

- Can become strongly attached to one parent in particular.

- May have tantrums when frustrated.

- May suffer separation anxiety and is upset when you leave the room – this can become more heightened at 18 months.

- Understands her own name and simple commands such as 'bring that to mummy'.

- Starts running, climbing and walking up and down stairs holding on.

- Likes listening to stories.

- Has vocabulary of about ten words by 18 months and can understand a lot more than she can say.

TWO TO THREE YEARS

- May have dreams and nightmares.

- May become fearful of the dark.

- Resists parents' requests.

- Becomes more independent.

- Moves to a bed.

- Reduces, and may stop napping completely.

THREE TO FOUR YEARS

- Starts to be dry in the night, so can come out of night nappies.

- Understands rewards.

- Can wait for short periods.

- Usually responds to limit setting.

- Asks lots of questions.

- Starts nursery

FOUR TO FIVE YEARS

- Starts school.

- Is very energetic and can be silly at times.

- Can express her anger in words.

- Has a better understanding of the concept of time and daytime activities such as dinner time and bedtime.

- Can understand and follow rules.

- Is starting to understand the feelings of others.

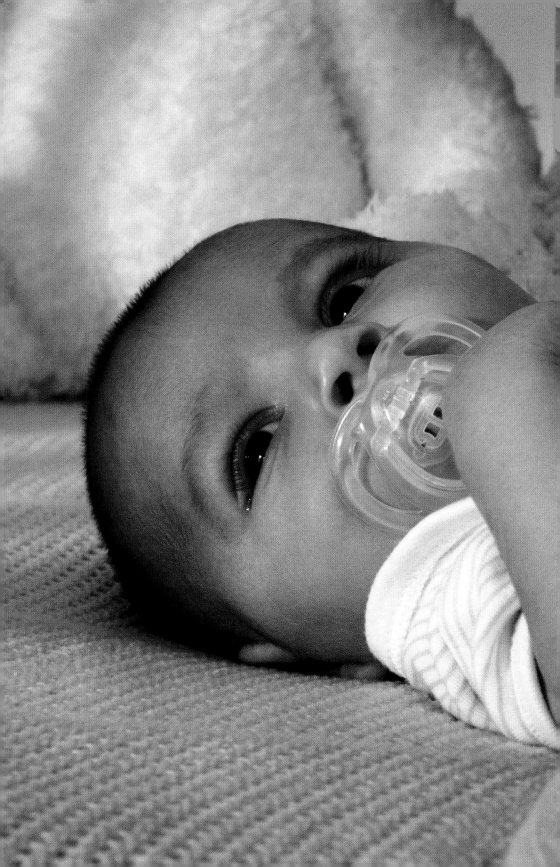

Encouraging
good sleep
habits

Helping your young baby into a good sleep rhythm

There are many successful ways to resolve an existing sleep issue, but it is even better if you can prevent difficulties developing in the first place. Research has shown that a significantly smaller percentage of babies have trouble settling or with night-waking when parents have gradually, and gently, introduced a routine early on.

The first three months

Before birth a baby is not aware of light and spends most of his time asleep, only waking for two to three hours a day in the last trimester. His sleep is regulated by your movement and melatonin (sleep hormone), which comes via the placenta. From birth to three months, his body clock and hormone production start to develop.

Your newborn will spend an average 16 hours a day asleep – his sleep is split roughly 50:50 between the day and night. At this stage his sleep is governed by his need to feed and since his tummy is so small, sleep episodes will be brief and he will wake every two to three hours for milk.

By ten weeks most babies can tell the difference between day and night and there are steps you can take to help him (see opposite). By three months they will sleep much more at night than in the day, and night-time sleep is in longer chunks, possibly five or six hours at a time. By now your baby's own melatonin production helps him sleep, and his day-and-night rhythms are in place.

Calming your baby

Your child's brain grows and develops faster in the first two years than at any other time in his life. The experiences that promote this process begin immediately – everything he hears, sees, touches, smells and tastes stimulates his brain to create billions of new pathways.

Ensuring that he has a stimulating environment will give him plenty of opportunities to learn and develop. But this needs to be balanced with quiet, calm time in familiar settings and predictable routines. If your baby becomes fussy and hard to calm, take him to a quiet room and hold, gently rock, stroke and sing to him. Talking out loud, for example, asking him what might be wrong with him, helps him feel he is being listened to from an early age. This approach also leads to calming hormones being released, laying down the foundation for good self-regulation.

The sleep cues

Here are some of signs, or cues, of tiredness you will see in your baby:

- Whining or fussing
- Staring blankly into space
- Frowning
- Jerky arms and legs
- Arching of back
- Clenched fists

- Yawning
- Rubbing eyes
- Pulling at ears
- Sucking on fingers or fist
- Ignoring interaction and losing interest

Soothing your young baby to sleep

By helping your baby feel safe and secure you can increase the chance of a better night's sleep. The womb was a noisy place, so some young babies are soothed by 'white noise'; you can download free white-noise apps and/or gently singing, humming or making a 'shushing' sounds works too. Young babies are also soothed by smell and find it comforting to be cuddled or rocked to sleep in the early weeks especially if they are agitated.

From around four to six weeks start trying to put your baby down when he is drowsy rather than fully asleep, keeping an eye on the time and looking out for sleep cues (below) to avoid your baby becoming overtired and harder to settle.

Then when you are ready, help your baby to understand that having a quiet and winding down bedtime bath and being gently dressed in different night-time clothes in the evening means it is nearly time to sleep.

Why a bedtime routine helps

Establishing a bedtime routine that encompasses multisensory stimulation has been clinically proven to increase the quantity and duration of your baby's sleep and result in fewer sleep problems. It needs to comprise various activities that together gently stimulate all your baby's senses and you should follow the same order every night before sleep. Research shows that the younger the baby is when a routine is initiated, the better. See Creating a sleep routine, pages 30–31).

For a multisensory routine that gently stimulates your baby begin with a warm bath, follow with a massage, then some quiet time, such as reading a book or singing a lullaby.

- Tactile – skin-to-skin contact during a bath and massage time

- Visual – make direct eye contact

- Auditory – he hears his parent's voice

- Smell – familiar scents of a parent

Baby massage

Giving your baby a massage as part of his daily bedtime routine will not only help to relax and soothe him but it could also help his sleep. Research has shown, after a month, babies massaged with lotion fell asleep faster, stayed asleep longer and woke less during the night.

Teaching your baby the difference between night and day

As light has the biggest influence on the body clock, you can help your baby to start the process of concentrating their sleep into the night by taking him outside every day for some fresh air and a dose of daylight. By day immerse your baby in the hustle and bustle of normal life. Studies have shown that newborns who were active at the same time of day as their parents were quicker to develop their body clock.

Combining the effects of daytime light with the soporific effects of darkness you will help your baby on the journey to learning that night-time is for sleeping. When you put your baby in his baby basket for his daytime nap, leave the curtains open and do not try to minimize noise. In contrast, keep the bedroom dark at night. And during night feeds, keep your voice low and eye-contact minimal to avoid overstimulating him; only change his nappy if it is really necessary.

How you can tell if your baby needs to sleep

Long before your baby talks, he will use non-verbal cues to tell you what he wants. He may have very subtle cues that tell you he needs sleep, and will progress quickly from being happy and playful to being tired and fussy.

In the first few weeks when there is little pattern to his sleep, being aware of the sleep cues can really help. Often the very first signs that your baby needs sleep is when he becomes quiet and still after a period of wakefulness. Now is the time to reduce stimulation and start settling your baby. In some babies the cues are very subtle and if you miss them your baby can become fractious, and be hard to settle. He will find it much easier to fall asleep if you are able to respond to those early sleep cues.

Creating a sleep routine

Sleep hygiene is the combination of the habits and practices, including a bedtime routine, that take place to prepare the brain and body for a good night's sleep. Good sleep hygiene helps optimize sleep onset and duration and is an important skill to learn. It's the foundation on which the healthy sleep habits of a lifetime are built and research shows it is best started early.

Establishing and maintaining a good sleep routine is important as it eases your child's body and brain through the transition from the fun and excitement of daytime activities into the preparation for a good night's sleep. It takes commitment and consistency so it is best for you and your partner to decide on a simple bedtime routine that you can both stick with for years to come.

Make sure the routine is both relaxing and enjoyable so your little one looks forward to her bedtime. The length and timing of your bedtime routine are as important as its constituents. The routine itself should be no longer than 45 minutes – 30 minutes is often ample.

It is important to do it at the same time everyday and at a time when your child is sleepy, but not overtired. Keep it focused around the bathroom and the bedroom your baby or child is sleeping in; going back into the play area or kitchen can give your child a confusing message that can result in her losing her focus for sleep.

What time is bed?

First, set a bedtime and aim to keep it the same every night. Research has shown this to be the key factor in ensuring young children have good-quality sleep; children who have a bedtime after 9.00pm have less sleep than those who are asleep before 9.00pm.

- Work out what time you would like to get your child up in the morning and the average amount of sleep she needs for her age – then set her bedtime.

- Consider the time of your child's last nap. Is it too close or too far away from bedtime?

- Do you need a routine based on your child's nursery or school start times?

Advantages of a bedtime routine	
	- It reduces night-time waking.
	- It takes less time for your baby or child to fall asleep and she will sleep for longer.
	- It sets up the expectation of sleep; as soon as you start the routine your child knows sleep is coming.
	- It provides an atmosphere of familiarity, warmth and security for your child that is conducive to calm rest.
	- It helps to regulate your child's sleep/wake cycle, or circadian rhythm.
	- It gives your child a sense of involvement and encourages cooperation.
	- It sets up positive sleep associations.

- Are you and your partner both going to be involved in bedtime – does this mean putting your child to bed later to accommodate this?

Bedtime routines

Families favour different bedtime routines, but there are important elements to include to ensure multisensory stimulation (see page 29).

Sleep schedule It is important that your child not only goes to bed at the same time each evening, but just as important that she wakes up at the same time every morning. A consistent wake-up time resets the 24-hour body clock to maintain your child's natural circadian rhythm.

Wind-down time Help your child quieten her busy brain an hour before sleep so avoid lively, vigorous play and chatting in the lead up to bedtime.

Exercise Children may struggle to sleep if they have been inactive during the day. Encourage her to have at least 30 minutes of exercise every day, but not too close to bedtime. Research shows muscles need a good two hours to cool down before sleep.

Screen time Turn off screens at least an hour before sleep. Not only is the content stimulating, but numerous studies have shown the blue/green light emitted by screens prevents the production of the sleep hormone melatonin.

Food and drink To avoid indigestion and early morning soiled nappies, give your child her last meal two hours before sleep time. If milk forms part of your child's bedtime routine, try offering this in a quiet room with a cuddle before you start. If your toddler needs a snack avoid anything containing caffeine and/or sugar.

Darkness Pre-dim the bedroom lights so, after her bath, your child returns to a darkened room. If she needs a night light, use one with a warm orange or red colour that will not interfere with her sleep.

Start quiet time an hour before bedtime.

Bathtime Bathe her for only five minutes in a warm bath and go straight from there into the dimly lit bedroom. Not only does this keep bathtime calmer, but the drop in body temperature after a bath, along with the darkened bedroom, will send a message to her brain that it is time for sleep, triggering the production of melatonin.

Straight to bed Keep the routine between the bathroom and the bedroom – avoid your play area or kitchen, for example, so you don't lose the magic and confuse your child.

Massage, cuddles, story and goodnight Massages, cuddles, stories, songs and lullabies are all good calming and enjoyable elements that will help your child recognize their sleep is coming. Follow with a cuddle and kiss goodnight.

Naps

Daytime naps are vital to babies and just as important as the sleep they get at night. In fact, 30 per cent of a three-month-old baby's sleep occurs in the daytime. Although nap time declines with age, the reduction is very gradual and even at the age of nine months many babies are still relying on naps for 20 per cent of their sleep.

Naps confer a number of concrete benefits for your baby:

- He will sleep better at night.

- He will have a better appetite, particularly soon after a nap.

- He will be happier and easier to manage.

- Having a regular daytime sleep routine will make a bedtime routine easier.

- Memory consolidation takes place during naps.

Spacing – the key to good naps

A significant proportion of your baby's sleep will come in the day, and it is as important to focus on the time between naps as on the length. If you space the naps well, the nap time should take care of itself. It is best to space them evenly through the day so that your baby naps well when the time comes instead of struggling to sleep because he is overtired or not tired enough.

Naps can be difficult to space out when daily activities cause your baby or toddler to nod off at the 'wrong' time, for example because you are out in the car or with the buggy.

A nap too late in the afternoon is likely to cause problems at bedtime, while a very early morning one can contribute to early rising. You can alter nap times but it needs to be done gradually over a few days by moving the start of the nap forwards or backwards by 15 minutes per day.

Children only sleep for certain number of hours out of every 24, so too much in the day may mean less sleep at night. The extra daytime sleep comes off the night in one of three ways: your baby may take a long time to fall asleep, be awake for a long period in the night or just wake too early.

If your baby struggles to nap or you feel you need to change your child's napping schedule, it can help to introduce a pre-nap routine. This doesn't need to be as rigid or as long as the night-time one, but could include toys away, a quiet drink, a look at a book and a cuddle. If you keep it brief, relaxing and consistent it will help your little one settle. Aim for your child to have at least one of his naps in his cot or bed, it is fine to have others on the go.

Understanding naps

A nap sleep cycle is around 30 minutes for a young baby and 45 minutes for an older one. You may find that sometimes your baby only sleeps for one cycle, while on other occasions his naps will be two or more cycles long. Do not be concerned if your baby always wakes after one cycle, he still benefits from napping.

When your baby is old enough to stay awake happily for two hours or more, it can help to balance his day by having the longest nap after lunch.

Bear in mind if you are making adjustments to your baby's nap times he will usually take longer to settle into them than for night-time changes. You will need to persevere for a couple of weeks to see signs of improvement – just trying something for a day or two will not be a fair reflection of your hard work.

Spacing naps in young babies Some babies want to snack and nap, but do not get enough food to last them until the next mealtime, nor enough sleep to give them the energy to enjoy a wakeful period. There are two ways to approach this:

1 Try increasing the time between naps. For example, if you want your baby to have a nap every three hours, but he cannot stay awake

Don't ...

Don't let your child nap later than 3.30pm from around nine months Sleeping on into late afternoon can reduce his sleep drive, making it more difficult for him to settle.

Don't give your child any stimulating food or drinks in the evening This includes drinks such as tea, coffee and cola, as well as sugary foods and cereals. Caffeine and sugar are stimulating and both negatively impact on sleep.

Don't give your child's his last meal just before bedtime You may think it will make him sleep more, but he is more likely to wake in the early evening with indigestion or early in the morning with a dirty nappy.

Don't create a bedtime routine that relies on props or triggers When your child wakes at night, he may want them to be repeated so he can get back to sleep (see Inappropriate sleep-onset associations, page 53).

Don't bring your child into the living area during or after his sleep routine This breaks the focus and sends confusing messages to your child.

Don't give your child a handheld device to watch at bedtime Not only will the screen's blue/green light stop melatonin production but the content may excite him when you are trying to calm him. It is best to stop all screens an hour before sleep.

Don't give in to extra requests from your child after saying goodnight. Allowing another drink or another trip to the toilet can become a delaying tactic and a habit. Where possible try to pre-empt it instead, or set boundaries by giving your child an established number of bedtime passes (repeat returns to bed) per night and stick to them.

Don't chat with your child if he wakes in the night Be as boring as possible and only say as much as you have to. It is best to have your discussions in the morning instead.

Don't discuss difficulties relating to your child's day at bedtime This may trigger anxieties or excitement that interferes with sleep; they are best discussed in the daytime. Try having five minutes of one-to-one talking time each evening after teatime instead (see page 87).

Don't send your child to his bedroom as a punishment Your child needs to feel that his bedroom is a place of harmony and rest.

more than two, delay the nap by 10–15 minutes every two to three days until you reach the desired time. Be consistent with your pre-nap routine and your method of settling your baby. If he becomes very overtired, slow down the process until he is ready to move on again.

2 If your baby falls asleep at the start of his feeds, try winding him or changing his nappy to rouse him. Offer him more of his feed when he seems more alert. Feeding times should improve as he has better daytime sleep.

Naps and night-time
There is a popular myth that by reducing the length or number of daytime naps, you will lengthen the night-time sleep or reduce the number of times your baby or toddler wakes in the night. This idea is particularly appealing to parents who have suffered broken nights over a long period or whose child wakes up very early. But it does not work.

A baby or toddler who is sleep-deprived in the day is likely to become cranky and overtired. This will not only make your bedtime routine more difficult, but it is also likely to impact on the quality of your child's night-time sleep. Levels of the wake-up hormone cortisol rise in the morning and decline during naps. Conversely, its level will creep up if a child is deprived of sleep, with the result that the child will have a less restful night and is likely to wake early. The faithful adage 'The more you sleep, the better you sleep' applies to naps as much as to nocturnal sleep.

Napping well leads to good night-time sleep.

Number and length of naps

All children are individual and mature at different rates, these are general guidelines:

- **Birth to four months** A young baby's naps will be spread throughout the day. On average she will need to sleep every 45 to 90 minutes. By three months her total daily nap time will be an average of five to six hours.

- **Four to six months** During this stage the time your baby can happily stay awake between naps will lengthen to two to two and half hours and she will have three or four regular naps a day. By six months, the total nap time averages three to four hours.

- **Six to nine months** During these months your baby's naps will reduce to two naps per day. At six months a baby will often have two naps of about 45 minutes each in the morning and late afternoon, plus a 90-minute sleep around lunchtime. By nine months, your baby will drop her late afternoon nap and her total daily nap time average will be two to three hours.

- **Nine months to one year** She is now down to two naps, one of about 45 minutes in the morning and another of one and half to two hours after lunch. To 'protect' her bedtime your baby needs to be awake by 3.30pm. By one year, the average daily nap time is two to three hours.

- **One year plus** The morning nap is usually dropped at this time, leaving just one midday nap, but this may be as long as two to three hours. Toddlers are often not tired enough for a morning nap, but become too tired to wait until after lunch, but you can easily solve this problem by temporarily bringing lunch forward (see Napping too much, opposite).

- **Two to three years** A single one-to-two hour nap is usually sufficient throughout this period. Many children will have grown out of naps altogether by the age of three years and will instead have an after lunch rest and wind down instead.

Most children no longer need a nap once they turn 3 years old.

Napping problems

Many parents have concerns about naps and can encounter problems. The most common are outlined below, together with some tried-and-tested solutions.

The short-napper Some babies settle well for naps, but then wake after a brief sleep. If this is familiar and your baby wakes happily from a short nap, then this pattern is what suits her right now. However, if she wakes crying and is grumpy and unhappy for a while, this suggests she is still tired and would benefit from sleeping longer (see Spacing – the key to good naps, page 32). Improvements can take a week or more so it is better to work on one nap at first – the lunchtime one is ideal because it needs to be longer.

- Keep a diary of your baby's nap schedule, taking note of the length of her naps (see Keeping a sleep diary, page 70–71).

- If your young baby wakes regularly after 30 minutes, go to her at 20 minutes (a timer can be useful). Listen out for signs of stirring, and try to pre-empt her waking by stroking, singing or gently rocking her in her cot. If she wakes fully, pat or rock her back to sleep. In time, she should take longer naps without your help.

- If you are following a sleep programme and your baby wakes prematurely from a nap, use the same procedure that you use to settle her at bedtime.

- For an older baby or child, wait a minute or two when she wakes – she may settle herself back to sleep.

- You may find setting up white noise close by will help dull any sharp sounds.

- If your baby is not asleep again within 20 minutes, abandon the nap to avoid upsetting the entire day's schedule.

Napping too much If your child is napping more than necessary for her age, it may affect her night-time sleep. For example, she may have difficulty falling asleep at bedtime, she may be awake for long periods in the night or she may wake too early. The amount of sleep that she gets

If your child has a late afternoon nap she may find it hard to fall asleep at her usual bedtime.

in 24 hours may not change, but more of it will have shifted to the daytime.

Napping too early If your child wakes too early in the morning, having a very early morning nap can perpetuate her early rising; it is as if part of the night-time has split away and become a nap. Try shifting this first nap by ten minutes each day until it is closer to the time she would normally nap if she woke up after 6.00am.

The transition from two to one nap a day after 12 months is one that toddlers often find difficult. Try cutting down the morning nap by 10 minutes each day, and moving the afternoon nap to just after lunch to help your child adjust. You could also try offering her a ten-minute power nap mid-morning as this will help to keep her going until she reaches nap time.

Creating the right environment for sleep

For the first six months your baby will be sleeping in your room, so creating the right environment for his sleep may help your sleep too. A sleep-friendly bedroom should be cave-like-quiet, cool and dark. When it comes to moving your little one into his own room ensure you recreate the same environment there too. Keep it simple, as this makes it easier to create the same sleeping conditions for him if you are away from home.

Noises off

Parents often worry that noises in or outside the house disturb their child's sleep. However, babies tend not to be as distracted by ambient noise as adults and, in general, once a baby or toddler is asleep it takes more than a thunderclap to wake them. Older children are a little more sensitive. Nevertheless, it is still not a good idea to creep about, because relative silence is likely to make your child more sensitive to noise.

If you live on a busy road, you are probably used to the constant hum of traffic; the same will apply to your baby. It can be like the 'white noise' produced by a vacuum cleaner or washing machine that young children often find soothing. As your child gets older and wakes more readily to the sound of aircraft, slamming doors, or your older child playing nearby, try dulling it with white noise. You can download apps onto a device and play them for the duration of the nap or at night to help mask sharp sounds.

Turn down the heat

Everyone sleeps best in a bedroom that is cool, but not cold. To the reduce the risk of sudden infant death syndrome (SIDS) the ideal room temperature for a baby is 16–20°C (60–68°F). He also needs light bedding or a lightweight, well-fitting baby sleep bag (see Safe sleeping, page 38–39).

Lights out

The main trigger for the release of the sleep hormone melatonin is darkness. So ensure your baby sleeps overnight in a darkened room from the age of about three months. If your room is naturally very light you may need to invest in lined curtains or black-out blinds. As a temporary measure bin liners or tin foil do a very good job.

Once your child is at the age where he finds everything around him distracting and exciting, you may find he sleeps better in a darkened room during the day too. Until then he does not need to nap in the dark.

The room does not have to be pitch black. A small red or amber nightlight will not impact on melatonin levels; these are particularly useful if your child is afraid of the dark. However, it is well-documented that the blue/green light from screens and hand-held devices impacts on melatonin levels and so our ability to sleep. Switch off all screens at least an hour before bedtime.

A small red or amber nightlight left on all night may help your child overcome a fear of the dark.

Common sleep problems

Common sleep problems and their causes

Although every child with a sleep problem exhibits it in her own way, the underlying causes fall into a small number of general categories.

Sleep disruptions can originate from a variety of factors. For example, they may arise because a child has never learned to go to sleep by herself, or because her sleep pattern has been recently disturbed by an illness, teething, holiday or the arrival a new baby. In their efforts to encourage their child to sleep, parents may be inadvertently perpetuating their child's night-time behaviour.

Your child's own stage of development – and any difficulties she may experience on the way – will influence if and how sleep problems first emerge. The three factors that can sustain or limit them are: what happens during the day; how bedtime is handled; and what happens when your child wakes at night.

Daytime napping Babies and young children need to nap during the day. However, if naps are at the wrong time or of the wrong length, sleep problems may occur at bedtime, later on in the night or cause early rising issues (see pages 32–35.).

Bedtime problems Settling a child for sleep often determines the course of the night to come. Problems at bedtime can be a common source of night-time disruption (see Creating a sleep routine, pages 30–31, and Inappropriate sleep on-set associations, opposite).

Night-waking All children wake in the night, however briefly. Waking is not the problem – it is your child's ability to get back to sleep unaided that makes the difference between a calm night and a disturbed night for both you and your child (see opposite).

Hunger in the night It goes without saying that babies need to feed at night. However, if your toddler or older child is still requesting milk or food in the night, she may have a night-time hunger habit that is no longer biologically necessary and but is the cause of frequent night-waking (see Sleep strategies, pages 74–76).

Nightmares and night terrors These are sleep disturbances that involve actual or apparent anxiety for the child. These are sporadic and unpredictable episodes, to be managed as and when they occur (see pages 54–57).

Pain or illness This can be the start of a sleep problem for a child who has previously slept well (see pages 46–49).

Lying with your child while she falls asleep may mean she needs your help to get back to sleep in the night.

Inappropriate sleep-onset associations

Getting your baby or child to sleep is not always the calm, idyllic process parents imagine. In reality, many parents find themselves resorting to on-the-spot aids to get their little ones to sleep, which their child comes to rely on. They might rock or stroke their child or lie down with her. Other possibilities include letting her fall asleep in their bed, or with the TV on, music playing, or a light on, or singing and whispering to her until she sleeps.

If your child has learned how to fall asleep this way, you will often find yourself repeating these conditions nightly at bedtime and again every time she rouses. These inappropriate sleep-onset associations are not uncommon and one of the most frequent causes of night-waking in babies and children. Research shows they are most common in the six to 36-month age group, but can occur in younger or older children. They can be learned from birth or can start after an upheaval such as a holiday, teething or an illness, when you have needed to give your child extra attention each time she woke up.

Parents often focus on the night-waking as the problem, not realizing that this is a symptom of their child's dependence on the sleep triggers. For example, if your child needs you to stroke her back to get to sleep at bedtime, she will want you to repeat this at night.

Typically, the first wake up is about two to three hours from your when your child fell asleep. As the night goes on they can be closer together, often at the end of a sleep cycle, so can be every 90 minutes.

In the early part of the night your child is likely to go back to sleep within a few minutes if you replicate what you did at bedtime. However, as the night progresses both the sleep hormone melatonin and the sleep-drive reduce, making it increasingly difficult to get your child back to sleep. Eventually your child may resist going back to sleep altogether and start her day early.

Preventing or stopping the association

Establish a regular bedtime routine and keep the conditions by which your child falls asleep consistent throughout the night. You may find some of the techniques in Chapter 4 useful, in particular check Sleep habits – Dos and don'ts, pages 48–49). Your child will initially take longer to go to sleep. However, it is worth persisting as you will both sleep better and gain confidence and independence.

Does your child have inappropriate sleep-onset associations?

It can be difficult to know whether your child is waking because of inappropriate sleep-onset associations or because something else is disturbing her. Signs of the former include:

- Inability to settle unless specific, familiar conditions are met.
- Frequent night waking.
- Inability to settle herself when she rouses at night
- Ability to return to sleep quickly once a prop is put back in place.

Sleep disorders and parasomnias

Sleep-walking, sleep-talking, confusional arousal, night terrors and nightmares are all behaviours that happen at night. They are very common in pre-school children, with more than 80 per cent experiencing what are known as parasomnias. They are harmless but can be upsetting and frightening for parents and children.

Night terrors and sleep-walking, the most common childhood parasomnias of non-rapid-eye movement (NREM) sleep, happen mainly in the first half of the night. Whereas rapid-eye movement (REM) sleep parasomnias, such as nightmares, tend to occur later in the night or towards the morning. Most of these disturbances are usually manifestations of a maturing neurological system or simply just run in your family. However, some are exacerbated by sleep deprivation, so ensuring your child gets all the sleep he needs will help.

Confusional arousal

An episode that starts with your child crying and thrashing around in bed. He may seem awake and upset, resists your cuddles and is difficult to wake. It lasts up to 30 minutes, but once it is over your child will calm and go back into a deep sleep.

Sleep-talking

This is common and tends to occur in the early stages of deep sleep, in the first third of the night. It is harmless, but can be annoying for anyone sharing a room with the talker; most children will grow out of it.

Sleep-walking

Also known as somnambulism, this is common – between seven and 15 per cent of children experience it and most will grow out of it. It is thought to be more prevalent in childhood as children have more deep NREM sleep.

Sleep-walking usually occurs about an hour after bedtime, when your child has entered NREM sleep (see pages 16–17) during which their brain is asleep but their body is mobile. There is no set pattern: it can last for five minutes or 20, and your child is usually calm. It often runs in families; a recent study found children are three to seven times more likely to sleep walk it if one or both parents have a history of it, but sleep deprivation can also be a trigger. While sleep-walking is a harmless, you may need to take measures to prevent your child hurting themselves in the process (See Solution 11, pages 136–137).

Rhythmic movement disorder (RMD)

As any parent who has had a toddler in bed with them will have learned, young children do not stay still when asleep. In children with RMD, this tendency is taken a stage further; symptomatic movements include recurrent head-banging, head-rolling and body-rocking, lasting from a few minutes to as much as an hour, that can easily disrupt the sleep of other family members.

Research shows RMD is very common in infants; up to 60 per cent of nine-month-olds will rhythmically move their body to get to sleep. Most children will outgrow RMD by the age of four years. RMD is normal in typically developing children and is a learned behaviour that a child uses to get themselves to get to sleep – at bedtime and during the night. Parental anxiety can inadvertently reinforce RMD if they soothe their child to sleep at bedtime or by waking them during an episode. The child soon connects his parents' presence with sleep onset and requests the same help to get back to sleep when he naturally wakes at night.

As RMD can co-exist with restless leg syndrome and obstructive sleep apnoea, or OSA (below), it is important to talk to your doctor about it to rule out these conditions.

As with all sleep disorders it is important to have a calm bedtime routine and a regular sleep/wake schedule. White noise can help dull the rocking sound. If your child is sleeping in a bed it may be best to place their mattress on the floor away from walls to prevent injury.

Snoring

This can be a normal symptom of a cold or virus in children, but when snoring persists and you notice other symptoms such as gasps or pauses in breathing, it could indicate a condition called obstructive sleep apnoea (OSA). OSA causes an obstruction of the airway during sleep and the child stops breathing for a few moments. During sleep the muscles in the throat relax. If your child has enlarged tonsils or adenoids this can cause a narrowing of their airway and reduce airflow. If your child's throat closes completely, he will stop breathing for a short time; oxygen levels drop and carbon dioxide levels rise. The rise in carbon dioxide signals your child to take a breath and he responds by taking a large gasp. As a consequence he will experience many brief arousals throughout the night and excessive daytime sleepiness. OSA affects one in 30 children, peaking at two to eight years of age. They are more susceptible if they are overweight, have Down's syndrome or there is a family history of the condition.

Night-time symptoms include:

- Restlessness, sweaty sleepers.

- Laboured breathing.

- Sleeping in unusual positions, often with the neck hyperextended backwards.

- Bedwetting (although this is common in children with no OSA).

- Mouth breathing and bad breath.

Children with OSA are usually very tired in the day, and often fall asleep in the morning, which impacts their behaviour and concentration. Studies show it can lead to hyperactivity, poor school performance, developmental delay and learning difficulties.

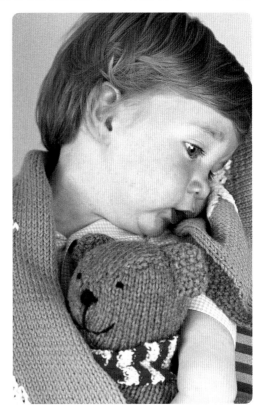

OSA (obstructive sleep apnoea) peaks at 2–8 years.

If you are concerned about your child, talk to your doctor. If they feel your child has OSA they will refer them for assessment, which may include an overnight sleep assessment called polysomnography. It may help if you take a phone video of your child sleeping and get notes from your child's school or nursery about their daytime behaviour. The British Lung Foundation is an excellent source of information and has a downloadable form that you can complete and take to your doctor (see Resources, page 156).

Nightmares and night terrors

Both these forms of sleep disturbance sound equally distressing but, in fact, they are quite different (see pages 54–57). Although most nightmares and night terrors are usually nothing to worry about, if your child has several episodes that occur over a period of time, it is advisable to talk to your family doctor.

Nightmares These occur during REM or 'dreaming' sleep (see page 16), so usually happen in the second half of the night when REM sleep becomes more frequent. Nightmares are very common, especially in pre-school children, and are a sign of your child's developing imagination. They usually reach a peak between the ages of three and ten years, when about a quarter of all children have at least one a week. However, they can happen in children as young as two years old.

As most of us will remember, common themes of nightmares include fear of separation, for example being lost, or something scary such as being chased by a monster. While the themes are frightening, nightmares are perfectly normal reactions to the stresses and anxieties of growing up. They can also be linked to hearing scary stories or TV programmes.

When your child wakes from a nightmare she is likely to call out or come to you in some distress. Listen to her and reassure her that she is safe and that you are close by. Stay with her until she has calmed down and is ready to go back to sleep. She may like a night light left on and the door open. It is best not discuss the theme at the time, talk about it in the daytime when it is less scary.

If your child has repeated nightmares on the same theme, help her to think up a happy ending to take out the fear factor. If there is an event causing her to feel anxious, your reassurance could make all the difference to how she feels about it.

Reassure her that everyone has nightmares, and even though they are scary at the time, they are normal. It will help if you encourage her to discuss concerns with you. Check her story books and TV programmes as many traditional tales involve bears and witches. Let her have a friendly bedtime toy as a security object to cuddle overnight. Look around her bedroom from her viewpoint; teddies and dolls may look very different in the dark. Ensure, too, that she is having enough sleep for her age, as children are much more likely to have nightmares when overtired (see page 14).

Night terrors These usually occur in the first few hours of the night, during deep NREM sleep. Understandably night terrors are concerning for parents. Around three per cent of children experience them, usually between the ages of 18 months to seven years, and most have grown out by the time they reach puberty.

A young child experiencing a night terror appears to 'wake up' suddenly out of a deep sleep, often with a wide-eyed, frightened expression,

Causes and prevention of night terrors

- **Sleep deprivation** This is the most common trigger. A sleep-deprived child has a greater need for very deep sleep, which is when these events happen. Ensure your child is having the right amount of sleep for his age (see page 14).

- **Irregular sleep schedule** Regular daytime naps and consistent bed- and wake-up times will help to stabilize your child's sleep pattern (see Creating a sleep routine, pages 30–31).

- **Stimulants** Avoid food and drink containing caffeine and/or sugar as both can disturb your child's sleep.

- **Stressful events and illness** Both can lead to disturbed sleep and it is the lack of sleep that acts as a trigger for the night terror.

- **Night terrors run in families** If there is a family history of night terrors, your child has an 80–90 per cent chance of experiencing them.

and sometimes screaming loudly. She may even get out of bed and run around in a state of seemingly inconsolable anxiety.

Ironically, while night terrors may leave parents feeling anxious, they do not disturb the child. Although your child may look terrified, she is usually totally unaware of what is happening as she is in a deep sleep. Night terrors rarely lasts longer than ten minutes, and your best response is simply to keep your child safe, wait until it passes, then guide her back to bed. Do not attempt to wake her or to offer comfort or reassurance as he is more likely to be upset if woken.

If your child regularly experiences night terrors, rousing her from her deep sleep in the early part of the night may prevent it (see Scheduled stirring, pages 80–81). Keep a sleep diary (see pages 70–71) so you can monitor when they typically occur. See also Solution 19, I think my child may be having night terrors, pages 152–153.

Always comfort and reassure a child suffering from a nightmare.

Distinguishing a nightmare from a night terror

Nightmare

- A frightening dream during REM sleep

- Occurs in the second half of the night

- Your child is upset afterwards

- Your child may need time to calm and return to sleep

- Parents should reassure and comfort

- Your child often remembers the episode in the morning

Night terror

- A partial waking from deep NREM sleep

- Occurs early in the night

- Your child is calm afterwards

- Your child returns to sleep quickly afterwards

- Parents should do little or nothing

- Your child remembers little or nothing

Other problems affecting sleep

Some conditions that affect children in their early lives can interfere with sleep. Although they are not sleep problems in themselves, they can be the cause of pain, discomfort or anxiety that may prevent your child falling and staying asleep. As a result, you may have needed to give your child extra comfort and reassurance to enable him to sleep. Once the condition has been resolved you may find your child now has an underlying behavioural sleep issue as a consequence. Ideally ensure the medical condition is resolved, before addressing any sleep concerns.

Infant colic

Affecting ten to 30 per cent of infants under three months of age, colic is characterized by long periods of inconsolable crying that starts and stops without obvious cause. It can last for three hours or more a day and for three days or more per week. Typically, your baby's face will be a flushed, he will have excessive flatulence a distended abdomen, and will draw his legs up.

Colic can disrupt day and night-time sleep, but it often strikes in the evening, so can interfere with bedtime routines. Studies show that it puts a huge strain families and is linked with maternal depression.

Despite decades of research the origin and nature of colic remains unclear. It may be that the underdeveloped stomach is under strain, daytime stress is being released, or the act of crying results in the intake of air into the stomach, with consequent discomfort. The symptoms frequently start in the second week of life and can occur in both breast- and bottle-fed babies.

Unfortunately, there is no single effective treatment and often only time brings relief. Remedies that help some babies may not help others. Rhythmic movement, such as rocking and walking around, often helps. Gently rubbing his abdomen or patting his back while holding him

Limiting the effects of reflux

- Give your baby more frequent, smaller feeds or meals, rather than fewer, larger ones. If you are bottle-feeding, experiment with styles of bottle and teat to help reduce excess air intake during feeding.

- Hold your baby upright for 30 minutes after a feed and wind regularly during and after feeding. Similarly, allow enough time between his bedtime feed and putting him in his cot for food to settle.

- Avoid putting him in a car seat or laying him flat for nappy changing straight after feeds.

- Loosen tight clothes and nappies around your baby's tummy.

- Avoid exposure to cigarette smoke.

- Do not let your baby cry for too long as it can encourage regurgitation.

When vomiting could be a problem

There are a number of warning signs that may suggest a more serious underlying condition. Seek medical advice for any of the following;

- Frequent projectile vomiting.

- Bile- (green or yellow green) or blood- (red) stained vomit.

- Bloody or jet-black stools.

- Onset of regurgitation and/or vomiting after your baby is six months old or persisting after one year old.

- Distended abdomen.

- Chronic diarrhoea or severe constipation.

- Not gaining weight and/or refusing feeds.

- Excessive crying or irritability during or after feeds.

- Episodes of choking or 'blue' colouration.

- Lethargy.

across your forearm or up against your shoulder may relieve some of the discomfort. Often, trying to do something is less stressful than doing nothing. Once an episode has run its course, your baby is likely to be tired and ready to sleep. Colic can be extremely wearing for you and this is a time when you may need to call on some respite help from family and friends.

One consolation is that colic rarely persists beyond the age of three or four months. But the resulting sleep associations can become habitual and your baby may continue to rely on being held and/or rocked to sleep. If this happens, see Inappropriate sleep-onset associations, page 53, for ways to help your baby to learn new sleep associations.

Gastro-oesophageal reflux

This is a common condition characterized by effortless regurgitation of stomach contents after a feed or meal, in otherwise healthy babies. It usually begins before a baby is eight weeks old. Episodes can be very frequent (about five per cent of affected infants have six episodes or more each day). So-called 'silent reflux' is a condition where stomach contents reach the gullet (oesophagus) and the back of the throat and can also cause discomfort.

Reflux can create stomach pains rather like heartburn, which are more uncomfortable when your infant is lying down. This makes it harder for babies to both fall and stay asleep. From a medical point of view, reflux is not a problem provided your baby is gaining weight and is otherwise healthy, but it can badly disrupt his sleep. Reflux can be very worrying for parents, but it resolves in 90 per cent of babies before they are a one year old.

Try holding your baby upright for 30 minutes after feeds to ease symptoms of reflux.

A baby suffering from a food intolerance may be very unsettled.

Food intolerances and allergies

A food intolerance is not the same as a food allergy. An intolerance, or non-allergic food hypersensitivity, occurs when the body is unable to process an ingredient in a food – for instance, lactose intolerance is caused by the body not having enough of the enzyme lactase to break down and digest lactose. A food allergy is a reaction by the immune system (our body's defence against infection) in which it mistakenly treats proteins found in foods as a threat; food allergy can be potentially life-threatening.

The severity of allergies and intolerances varies widely, however, both can cause severe sleep disruption including restless, fractious sleep with frequent unexplained waking, shorter sleep cycles and dramatic reductions in total sleep time over 24 hours.

Studies indicate that around one in 12 young children suffer from a food allergy. The foods that most commonly cause intolerances and allergies in young children are cow's milk, eggs, soya, foods containing gluten, such as wheat, barley and rye, nuts, peanuts, seeds, fish and shellfish. Cow's milk allergy affects three to six per cent of children in the UK alone, although most outgrow it by the age of five.

The sheer variety of these symptoms combined with the delayed reaction to foods in the case of an intolerance, often mean you may not suspect a milk or food intolerance at first, or you may lack the proof that this is the cause. If you suspect your child has an allergy or intolerance you should talk to your doctor. They will also be able to advise you on what products to avoid and on suitable nutritional substitutes.

Food intolerance	• Can be caused by many different foods.
	• Symptoms come slowly, often many hours after eating the food.
	• Symptoms include nausea, gas, cramps, abdominal pain, diarrhoea, irritability, back arching and/or an itchy rash.
	• Child may be able to eat small amounts of the offending food without trouble, however, symptoms can occur after larger amounts of the food.

**Food
allergy**

- Symptoms come on very quickly after eating just a small amount of the food.

- Symptoms can be life-threatening.

Reactions can be very serious and consist of:

- Coughing, wheezing and shortness of breath.

- Swelling of lips, mouth and throat.

- Itchy skin and/or rash.

- Diarrhoea or vomiting.

- Runny or blocked nose and sore, red and itchy eyes.

Constipation

This will affect most children at some time in their childhood and the discomfort it causes in the lower abdomen is likely to disturb your child's sleep, but only until she is able to empty her bowel. It has no single identifiable cause, but insufficient fluid or fibre intake is a common contributory factor. Other common causes are worries or anxieties, such as starting nursery, moving home, the arrival of a new sibling or problems with potty training.

What you can do to help It is best to treat the constipation as soon as possible as the longer it persists, the longer it takes to resolve. Try modifying her diet before considering medication. This means increasing your child's intake of water and high-fibre foods, such as fruit and vegetables and unrefined cereal products. If this does not work within a few days, consult your doctor who may prescribe laxatives.

Encourage your child to sit on her potty or the toilet after meals and before bed. You may wish to set up a positive reward system if they manage a poo. Try to stay calm and not let your child see this as stressful for you – a smile and reassurance will help her see it in a positive light.

Ear infection

These are very common in children and often get better on their own within three days. However, the pain in the ear that accompanies them can disrupt your child's sleep.

You should take your child to see your doctor if the earache lasts longer than three days or she has a very high temperature (38°C/100.4°F or above), feels hot and shivery, there is swelling around their ear or fluid coming from their ear, or she has any other symptoms such as vomiting. If your child has a history of recurrent ear infections, it is worth checking with your doctor to make sure there is not a build-up of fluid (glue ear) in the middle ear as a result.

A diet higher in fibre and water can help to alleviate constipation.

Bed-wetting

It is common for children to go through a period of wetting the bed when they stop using nappies at night. It is part of the transition to nocturnal bladder control, which typically happens between the ages of three and four years.

However, children differ a lot in when they are able to stay dry at night, as it follows a complex process involving several developmental stages. The urinary system has to develop the ability to produce less urine at night, so that the bladder fills less quickly. Coordination has to develop between the nerves and the muscles that control the bladder. Also, your child has to learn to wake up when his bladder is full. Although all of this happens quite quickly in some children, it typically takes several months.

By the age of two and a half most children are dry during the day and, by three years old three-quarters of these children are also dry most nights. However, for many this is a slow learning process – and boys tend to be slower than girls. By the age of four years, one in ten children still wet their beds at least once a week. The older the child, the more anxiety bed-wetting tends to cause. This should be treated with patience and reassurance but also practical support (see below).

There is very little scientific evidence to back up the idea that bed-wetting is a psychological problem. Some children wet the bed if they have anxieties at home or school, but it is more often a cause, rather than the result, of unhappiness.

It can be stressful if you are regularly being woken at night to change bed sheets. Try to be patient – stay calm, change the bedding and get your child back into bed with minimal fuss. Until your child is regularly sleeping through the night without wetting his bed, it is probably best to use a waterproof cover on the mattress and have a supply of wipes, sheets and bed clothes handy.

Not all children will grow out of bed-wetting and some need additional help. It is recommended that children who are still bedwetting at the age of five years should be seen by a health care professional. The sooner your child is treated for bed-wetting the greater chance they have of becoming dry at night.

How you can help

- Encourage your child to have at least six drinks during the day. This helps to train the bladder to hold larger quantities and prevents excessive drinking in the evening.

- Restrict caffeinated drinks, such as cola, tea and coffee, as caffeine can irritate the bladder.

- Some parents like to lift their child on to the toilet before they go to bed (for instance, at about 11.00pm) to encourage them to pass some urine. This is not recommended as it may encourage a child to wee while he is half asleep, which can cause more accidents.

- Do not restrict drinks in the evening. If your child seems to want a lot of liquid in the evening, it is probably because he is not drinking enough in the day, so the best approach is to encourage daytime drinking.

- Consider offering a reward to an older child when she does not bed-wet to increase her motivation to stay dry.

Encourage your child to drink well in the earlier part of the day so she is well-hydrated and not overly thirsty in the run up to bedtime.

Reasons for bed-wetting There are a number of reasons for bed-wetting.

- Susceptibility to bed-wetting runs in families. If one parent had this problem, thelikelihood of a child doing the same is 40 per cent. This increases to 70 per cent if both parents had the problem.

- Your child may not wake when their bladder is full.

- Your child's bladder does not stretch enough to hold the volume of urine they make overnight.

- Your child's body may not produce enough of the hormone vasopressin that slows down the production of urine at night.

- Occasionally a medical condition such as a urine infection is responsible. See your doctor if you suspect this to be the case.

- Constipation can put pressure on the bladder.

- Children who do not drink much early in the day tend to compensate by drinking a lot in the evening and are then unable to retain the volume of fluid. You can encourage your child to drink at home. If she is at nursery or school, ask her teacher to encourage her to drink more.

When sleep problems seem difficult

Most babies and toddlers can sleep under the most hostile conditions: in a crowded or draughty room, or next to noisy road works. Young children seem able to do this whatever the situation. The innate capacity to sleep against the odds that babies and toddlers demonstrate daily, however, can be deceptive.

As with any other feature of your child's life, sleep patterns change and develop, often rapidly. Just when you are accustomed to your baby sleeping for four hours between feeds and waking once a night, she will switch to feeding every two to three hours and/or wake three times a night. Or your toddler will be napping conveniently after lunch for two hours and then suddenly start wanting to nap in the late afternoon instead. Adapting to such changes is all part of the parenting challenge; nevertheless, it can be confusing.

Mostly these changes are a perfectly normal response to a stage of your child's development or a change in circumstance, such as starting nursery. Whatever the cause of the sleep issue the resulting sleep deprivation can have profound consequences for both you and your child's physical and emotional health, so it is important to recognize the problem and, as soon as you can, take steps to resolve it.

To do this, it helps to have an understanding of which developmental stages could impact on your child's sleep (see Developmental stages and sleep, pages 20–25). By anticipating them, if the need arises, you will be able to nip an emerging problem in the bud.

What next?

Once you have identified that your child has a sleep problem the next big leap is doing

Spot the sleep problem!

Your child may have a sleep problem if she:

- is a young baby and has very short or very few naps in the day;

- is very groggy in the morning and sleepy during the day;

- seems overtired and is easily upset in the day;

- resists going into her cot or bed;

- takes a long time to fall asleep;

- seems anxious as bedtime approaches;

- has a bedtime that is getting later over a short period;

- keeps coming into the living area after you have said goodnight;

- can only fall asleep in your arms and wakes in the night to be resettled;

- often wakes in the night;

- is awake for long periods in the night;

- wakes up very early several times a week;

- has regular nightmares or night terrors.

something about it. But, before you embrace that challenge, consider how you want to approach it. Once you start to enquire, you will find plenty of advice, but it can be conflicting. Where do you start? Your doctor's advice to stop your toddler napping conflicts with your mother's advice to let her sleep as much as she wants in the day, which conflicts with advice on the parenting website to put her to bed earlier. What you need is simplicity and clarity from a trustworthy source. Remember though that there is not necessarily a solution for everybody and they should be always be adapted to your family and its circumstances, not the other way around.

Look after yourself

Parenthood is often our first encounter with sleep deprivation. Only then can you appreciate why it is successfully used as a form of torture! Parental sleep deprivation is clearly of a different order, but it can manifest itself in many insidious ways. For you, it may lead to a predictable doziness in the late morning; an afternoon slump in physical energy and concentration; or irritability that brings you close to tears in the evening. None of which are compatible with the demands of looking after a baby or toddler.

Tiredness can affect your mind as well as body, and almost all parents find that it makes them impatient and moody. Almost all parents find it affects their judgement and makes them impatient and moody. Those parents deprived of REM sleep, in particular, may find themselves less able to regulate their emotions, swinging quickly from very happy to sad, and becoming anxious and forgetful – symptoms that can be confused with low mood or even postnatal depression. Most REM sleep occurs in the second half of the night, so to help overcome your lack of this valuable sleep, try taking turns with your partner to do the morning shift.

Survival strategies

Identifying yours and your partner's chronotype (see pages 18–19) can help you cope better. If you are an owl you may find it easier to take the late evening shift and if your partner is a lark they may find they cope better with the early morning shift.

It is best to manage sleep problems as soon as they emerge.

Try to take a nap or have a rest when your baby is sleeping – even if you lie down with your eyes closed you may well fall asleep without realizing it.

Remember to eat! It is important to keep up your energy levels. Having small amounts of protein with every meal and as snacks will keep your blood sugar more constant. It is best to avoid sugary foods and caffeine as they might give you a quick boost, but your blood sugar levels will drop much faster.

Try taking your baby out for a good dose of afternoon light each day. This has been shown to help establish young babies' body clocks and will help you sleep better too.

Accept all offers of help from family and friends. And if you have an older child, arrange for him to be picked up from nursery or school some days. A local parent's support group could be an invaluable place to share tips and find sympathetic ears, and if you feel you are not coping do talk to your doctor or health visitor.

Addressing
sleep concerns

Ten key questions – assessing your child's sleep

You probably know what your child's sleep issue is, but, before you explore ways of addressing it, it is useful to consider some basic key questions. This will help you to isolate the issues that are causing concern and, together with the information from your sleep diary (see pages 70–71), will set you on target to sort it out.

Is your child well? Could your child's sleep disturbance be the result of an illness? Disturbed sleep can be the first sign of, for example, a cold or an ear infection. If so, the priority is to treat the medical condition, but it is also important to ensure that the short-term sleep disturbances do not become longer-term problems. The best way to do this is to try to maintain your child's bedtime routine as much possible during the illness, so that good sleep habits can readily be reinforced when your child is better.

How long has the problem been going on? Consider whether your child's sleep problem is of recent origin. Could it have been triggered by a particular event in his and the family's life, linked to his stage of development (see pages 20–25), or to sudden changes in his circumstances (see Times of change, pages 42–47) or his sleep routines?

How much sleep does your child have? Do you know if he is getting enough sleep, both in the daytime and at night for his age? Sleep problems are so disorienting that it can be difficult to remember exactly what has happened in the preceding days and weeks. Completing a sleep diary can help provide you with a clearer picture of what is going on (see pages 70–71). You can then compare this with typical expectations for a child of his age (see What to expect of your child's sleep, page 14–15).

How easily does he settle at night? A child's bedtime routine often sets the pattern for the night. Is he taking a long time to settle, and/or does he require sleep props or triggers that have become inappropriate sleep-onset associations (see page 53)?

Does your child have regular sleep routines? Irregular routines often underpin sleep problems. Are his day-to-day nap times and bedtime routine consistent? Again, with the aid of a sleep diary (see pages 70–71), you can identify whether his sleeping and waking times are regular. Establishing appropriate and consistent routines, if these are not already in place, is often the only measure you have to take to help your child sleep better.

Is night-waking an issue? Night-waking is a very common sleep problem, but understanding why it happens is the key to solving it. How often does your child wake up, how long is he awake for, and why does he wake? Check on the typical expectations for a child of his age (see page 14). What does it take to get him back to sleep? Does he need you or a sleep prop in order to get back to sleep? (See inappropriate sleep-onset associations, page 53).

Does your child experience sleep-related anxiety? Anxieties can prevent children settling well. They can be about a range of things, although fear of the dark or nightmares are probably the most common, and can be the cause of both bedtime and night-time sleep issues (see Creating the right environment for sleep, pages 36–37).

Does your child appear fearful if he wakes in the night and are you able to calm or reassure him? Alternatively, are his anxieties caused by other sources of stress that have then resulted in sleep problems? Does he thrash around or call out in his sleep? Does he sleep-talk or sleep-walk (see Sleep disorders and parasomnias, pages 54–57)?

What is your child's temperament like in the day? Lack of sleep very often has an impact on daytime mood and behaviour, which can impact on the whole family. Is your child sleepy when he gets up, or does he struggle to stay awake later in the day? What is his general mood? Is he irritable, is he easily upset or have problems concentrating on what he is doing? These can all be signs of the sleep deprivation that arises from sleep disruption. Parents frequently tell us that when their child's sleep improves so does their mood and behaviour.

Is the environment conducive to good sleep? Lots of things can potentially disturb a child's sleep patterns (see Times of change, pages 42–47). These changes may be unavoidable in the short term, however, as soon as you are in a more settled place, implement a plan to get your child's sleep back on track. The shorter the duration of the disruption, the quicker it will be resolved.

The physical environment in which your child sleeps is also important. Are the circumstances surrounding his bedtime routine calming? Consider temperature, noise, and light. Are your children sharing a room and could this be exacerbating his sleep difficulties? (See Chapter 2, Encouraging good sleep habits, pages 26–49.)

What solutions have you tried? Consider the techniques that you have tried before: how long you did you keep to the plans and to what extent did they work? Do not assume that a technique that you have already tried unsuccessfully will never work; its success can depend greatly on how and when you apply it.

(See also the flow charts in Chapter 5, Identifying the problem, pages 90–111.)

Keeping a sleep diary

When does your baby or child sleep and for how long? What influences or interferes with her pattern of sleep? Is the pattern repeated over successive days or weeks?

These are simple questions, but many parents would have difficulty answering them with any certainty, especially when they are busy and over-tired. However you will need this basic information to establish whether your child has a sleep problem and the best course of action. One of the best ways to record this is to keep a sleep diary.

Like the example below, this can be a very simple document, but the data that it provides can be used to address a whole host of sleep problems.

A diary enables you to:

- Assess whether your child is getting enough sleep and if this sleep is at the best times.

- Track your progress day-to-day. Whether you are introducing a full structured sleep programme or just making initial changes to meal and nap times, you will be better able to ascertain the impact of what you are doing.

- To be more objective about a problem that is often emotionally charged. With the bare facts, it is much easier to spot the emergence of patterns, which you can then address quickly.

Sample Millpond sleep diary for nine month old		Monday	Tuesday	Wednesday	Thursday
	Time wakes in morning	5.30am ❶	5.30am ❶	6.30am	6.20am
	Time & length of nap(s) in day	7.00–9.00am ❷ 12.00-1.00pm 4.00-5.00pm ❸	7.30-8.45am ❷ 12.00-1.00pm 4.00-4.30pm ❸	9.00-9.45am 1.30-3.00pm	9.30–10.15am 1.00-2.00pm 4.30-6.00pm ❽ ❸
	Time start prep. for bed in evening	6.00pm ❽ ❹	6.00pm ❹	6.00pm ❹	7.30pm
	Time went to bed in evening	7.00pm ❺	7.15pm ❺	7.00pm	8.30pm ❺
	Time went to sleep	8.00pm	8.30pm	7.15pm	9.30pm ❽
	Time(s) woke in the night; what you did; time(s) went to sleep again	10.30–10.45pm rocked to sleep in cot ❼ 2.00-2.45am fed	11.00-11.20pm rocked and put back into cot ❾ 3.00am fed 4.30–5.30am rocked back to sleep; awake for an hour ❿	10.00–10.20pm patted to sleep in cot ❼ 2.00am fed and into cot 4.30am fed and into parents' bed	12.15–12.30am rocked and put back into cot 4.00am fed and put back into cot ❾

- To see the connections between what your child is doing outside sleep times and if this affects her sleep.

- Assess your responses to your child's sleep habits, enabling you to see where you are genuinely helping or unintentionally hindering the problem.

- See baseline information against which you can assess not only changes in your child's behaviour but also your management of those changes.

- To remain consistent, which is especially important when trying to establish a routine.

- Show any health professionals you may consult.

- Increase your motivation by revealing small improvements in your child's sleeping habits when you have changed her routine.

When is the best time to start keeping a diary?
The answer is almost certainly today. Even if you have not decided how to manage your child's sleep, any information you gather now will give you a head start in determining which approach to take and subsequently how you are progressing.

You may also like to make a note of your aims on the diary page. Like a mission statement, this can keep you focused on your goal when you're tired and emotions clouds your judgement and threaten to throw you off course.

You may be surprised what a simple daily diary can teach you, and this knowledge will help you guide your child towards better sleep.

Friday	Saturday	Sunday
7.30am	6.30am	7.00am
10.00–10.45am ⑥ 1.30-3.00pm	9.30–10.15am ⑥ 1.30-3.00pm	10.15-11.30am 2.00-3.30pm ⑥
6.15pm ❹	6.00pm ❹	6.15pm ❹
7.15pm	7.00pm	7.15pm
7.30pm	7.30pm	7.30pm
11.15–11.50pm rocked and patted to sleep-into cot 3.00-3.30am fed and put back in cot	11.00–11.30pm patted and rocked, then into cot 2.00-2.45am rocked and into cot ⑨ 4.30am fed and stayed in parents' bed; awake for 90 minutes ⑩	4.30–5.30am fed and brought into parents' bed; awake for an hour ⑩

① Early rising may be contributing to multiple naps.

② The first nap is too early and is treated by your baby as night sleep.

③ At nine months most babies drop to two naps a day.

④ Bedtime is started too early compared with your baby's natural sleep time – one hour is plenty.

⑤ Your baby is taking a long time to go to sleep – the ideal time is closer to 15 minutes.

⑥ Better timed naps help the day flow well.

⑦ Your baby will go back to sleep much more quickly in the early part of the night due to his high sleep drive.

⑧ From nine months it is best to finish your baby's last nap by 3.30pm. Having a late nap may mean he struggles to fall asleep at bedtime.

⑨ Your baby needs your help to be able to get back to sleep in the night.

⑩ It is more difficult to get your baby back to sleep in the early hours of the morning.

Sleep strategies

You have probably turned to this page because you are struggling with lack of sleep and are concerned about the impact sleep deprivation may be having on your child. You are ready to address the issue and would like to consider which sleep strategies would suit your child and family, and how best to apply them.

What next?

Over the next few pages, we will explain some tried-and-tested, evidence-based sleep plans. To help you identify the nature of the problem you are experiencing and pinpoint the best plan and direction for you, refer to the relevant flow charts in Chapter 5, Identifying the problem (see pages 90–111). Then, to see how they work in action, look at the appropriate case studies in Chapter 6, Sleep solutions (see pages 112–155).

All the techniques work best if both parents are fully committed and ready to support each other. It is vital to choose a plan that you feel is not only right for your child's sleep issue and your parenting style, but that you also feel confident to take up. Each plan also depends on you establishing a regular and relaxing bedtime routine (see Creating a sleep routine, pages 30–31, and Sleep habits – Dos and don'ts, pages 48–49).

Gradual retreat plan

This is a very gentle and effective technique that can be adapted for any age group. It is based on the concept that parents can slowly reduce the assistance their child needs to help him go to sleep. The aim is to gradually wean your child off his sleep-onset associations. This approach gives your child time to adapt to the changes at his own

Before you go any further

There are a few factors you may wish to consider:

- There is no one size fits all approach – you can adapt most strategies to suit your child, your parenting style and your living conditions.

- Before you set out, work out what your goals are and whether they are realistic.

- You do not have to address everything at once – you can start with the easier fixes first and build from there.

- There is no quick fix, it takes time and consistency to see a change.

- In the beginning you may find you have less sleep than you have now.

- You and your partner both need to be committed and ready to make a change.

- Your child is fit and well and there are no medical factors that should be considered first.

- You have checked your support network to see who can help out if needed.

- Your diary is not packed with critical work deadlines or challenging events.

- You are doing this because you have decided to and you are not feeling under any pressure to make this decision.

- You have filled in a sleep diary for your child as a baseline from which to work (see pages 70–71).

pace until he is able to fall asleep by himself. Your starting point will always depend on how you currently settle your child to sleep.

Gradual retreat for a baby or toddler in a cot

How do you settle your baby or toddler to sleep now? Does he settle to sleep while:

- Feeding

- Being rocked or cuddled in your arms

- Being patted and 'shushed'

- You sit next to his cot

- He is in your bed with you

Step one Start your gradual retreat technique by settling your child to sleep moving to the next degree of physical closeness. For example, if you normally rock your child to sleep, your first goal is to settle him to sleep in your arms while you walk and pat him instead. When your child is settling well this way, move onto the next step.

Step two Your next goal is to stand still while cuddling your child, but rhythmically patting his thigh until he settles to sleep in your arms. Once he is settling well this way move to the next step.

Step three Your next goal is to place your child in his cot and pat him or stroke between his eyebrows. It will be less back breaking to sit beside the cot and put your hands through the bars. Once he has adapted to this, move on to the next step.

Choose a strategy to suit your parenting style.

Step four Now your goal is to settle your child in his cot with your hand lightly resting on his tummy or thigh. Once he has adapted to this move on to the next step.

Step five Your goal now is to settle your child to sleep in his cot with no touch, while you sit close by – offering verbal reassurance if needed. Once he has adapted to this, gradually move further and further away from the side of his cot until he can settle independently.

See also Solution 2 (pages 118–119) and Solution 13 (pages 140–141).

Gradual retreat plans

Throughout your gradual-retreat sleep plan aim to:

- Repeat each step for at least three to four nights (or longer), before you move on – it is important to go at your child's pace.

- Make minimal eye contact and limit your voice to sounds ('shush', 'sleepy time now', 'lie down, sleepy time').

- Make sure your child is fully asleep before you stop what you are doing – wait an extra ten minutes to be sure.

- If your child wakes in the night, use the same method you used at bedtime to settle him back to sleep.

- Keep a sleep diary to monitor the changes and 'see' your progress.

Gradual retreat for a child in a bed

How do you settle your child now – does she only falls asleep if you or your partner:

* Cuddle her, either in her bed or your bed;

* Sit on the edge of her bed;

* Sit on a chair next to her bed;

* Sit across the room, just to be seen.

Step one Start your gradual retreat by moving onto the next degree of physical closeness. So, for example, if you normally cuddle your child to sleep, your first goal is lie beside her side-by-side without cuddling. When your child is settling well this way, move onto the next step.

Step two Your next goal is to sit up on the bed until she settles to sleep. Once your child is settling well this way move to the next step.

Step three Your next goal is to sit with your feet over the side of the bed. Once she has adapted to this move on to the next step.

Step four Now your goal is to settle your child as you kneel or sit on a cushion beside her bed.

Choose a cushion you already have at home and call it 'sleepy cushion'; this cushion will act as a marker for where you will sit each night as your child goes to sleep. The goal now is for your child to settle herself to sleep while you sit on the 'sleepy cushion'. Once she has adapted well to settling while you sit on the cushion by the bed, gradually move it further and further away until your child can settle to sleep without you in her bedroom. See also Solution 8 (pages 130–131) and Solution 12 (pages 138–139).

Repeat each step for three to four nights, or longer, before you move on to the next step; just go at your child's pace. If your child is old enough you could use a reward system. This will help to reinforce the progress they have made and will make the experience more positive for your child (see Positive reinforcement – rewards, page 82).

Reducing night feeds for a baby over six months

Reducing the number of night-feeds, or weaning your older baby or child off them altogether, is a decision that should be made by you, without any influence or pressure from anyone else. You might want to do it because you are returning

Reducing feeds

Once you have made your decision, it is best to manage this process slowly and consistently. You may prefer to start by just making changes to your baby's bedtime routine as this alone will help the nights to improve.

* Offer her a feed at the start of her bedtime routine, rather than at the end. Do this in a quiet room to ensure she stays focused and feeds well.

* She may request another feed after her bath, but as this is likely to be small, she will still be awake when you settle her to sleep – this is a great first step towards supporting her to sleep independently. Over time you can aim to give your baby all her feed before her bath.

* So you know your baseline, for the next few nights record the time your baby or toddler wakes and how long each breastfeed usually is, or the volume of a bottle feed. If she feeds very frequently and takes a small amount each time, it is best to start by reducing the number of night feeds by spacing them out, see opposite. If your child is waking less frequently and taking a larger feed, start by reducing the volume (see page 76).

Schedule for spacing out feeds

You can decide how slowly to take this depending on you and your child – here are some guidelines.

Night	Time between breast- or bottle-feeds
1	2 hours
4	2.5 hours
8	3 hours
12	3.5 hours
16	4 hours

to work, having another baby, worried about the impact your lack of sleep is having on you and your family, or simply just feel now is the right time. It is perfectly normal for all babies to wake for night feeds for at least the first year. Your baby may not just waking because she is hungry, but for comfort, thirst or a way of getting back to sleep.

You do not have to stop *all* night feeds. You may feel you could cope better if your child woke less often, and would prefer to just reduce, or space out, her night-time feeds. Before making any changes to night feeds you need to take into consideration other factors, such as whether your baby is growing well and reaching her developmental milestones, and is she happily eating and drinking during the day.

See also Solutions 14, 15, and 16, pages 142–147.

Spacing frequent night-time feeds for a baby over six months This technique may suit you if your child is waking frequently for small feeds. You can reduce the number of feeds by gradually extending the interval between them.

- If your baby is waking every one-and-half hours, for example, you could aim initially to extend the gap to two hours.

- If your baby wakes before the two hours (or your desired gap), comfort and reassure her with cuddles and physical closeness until you reach your feed time or she goes back to sleep.

- Slowly increase the gap between the feeds by 15 to 30 minutes every fourth night until the feeds are spaced out by your desired goal, for example roughly three-to-four hourly.

Your baby may still be waking for feeds for at least the first year.

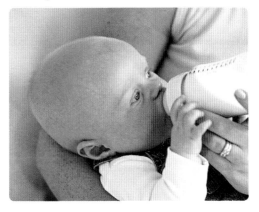

How to reduce a specific night breastfeed for babies over six months This technique may suit you if you wish to stop a specific feed. Work out your child's usual maximum feed length, for example 15 minutes, and aim to reduce it by one minute every one to three nights.

- On the first night, for example, feed him for no more than 14-minutes then gently remove him from your breast and settle him back to sleep, comforting and reassuring him with cuddles and physical closeness. If he takes less than the maximum feed time that does not matter and if he falls asleep feeding that's fine.

- Reduce the feed by one minute every few nights until it is about two or three minutes long. The following night do not offer a feed at this time, but instead settle him back to sleep with cuddles and physical closeness.

- You may find that for a few nights your child continues to wake around the time of his usual feed; this is quite normal, just settle him back to sleep as above.

How to reduce a specific bottle feed for babies over six months Work out your child's usual maximum feed or water volume, for example 150ml (5fl oz), and aim to reduce this by 20ml (^{3}$_4$fl oz) every other night.

- On the first night, for example, offer him a 130ml (4^1$_4$fl oz) bottle. When he has finished, gently remove it and settle him back to sleep, comforting and reassuring him with cuddles

Schedule for reducing night feeds	These are guidelines to help you but take it as slowly as you want; it very much depends on you and your child.	

Night	ml/fl oz per bottle	Minutes of breastfeeding
1	200ml (6^3$_4$fl oz)	14
3	180ml (6fl oz)	13
5	160ml (5^1$_2$fl oz)	12
7	140ml (4^3$_4$fl oz)	11
9	120ml (4fl oz)	10
11	100ml (3^1$_4$fl oz)	9
13	80ml (2^3$_4$fl oz)	8
15	60ml (2fl oz)	7
17	40ml (1^1$_4$fl oz)	6
19	No more night feed	5
21	No more night feed	4
23	No more night feed	3
24	No more night feed	No more night feed

Aim to start your routine only 30–40 minutes before planned actual bedtime. As you shift the sleep time forward then your child's spontaneous wake-up time will move as well.

Period	Bedtime
Starting sleep phase	5:30pm
Day 1	5:45pm
Day 4	6pm
Day 8	6:15pm
Day 12	6:30pm – new bedtime

and physical closeness. If he does not finish the bottle it does not matter, likewise if he falls asleep feeding that is fine.

- Once the feed is reduced to only 40ml (1¼fl oz), do not offer a bottle for this feed the following night. Instead settle him back to sleep with cuddles and physical closeness.

- You may find that for a few nights your baby continues to wake around the time of his usual feed. This is to be expected, just settle him back to sleep as above.

Resetting your child's body clock

You may feel your child is a night owl, if he takes a long time to go to sleep, eventually falling asleep an hour or two after you have said goodnight, and then he usually sleeps through the night but struggles to get up in the morning. Or, your child is an early morning lark if he usually falls asleep easily at bedtime, wakes spontaneously before 6.00am and has very little energy left come late afternoon. These patterns are often called late and early sleep phases, and the strategies used to resolve them lie in shifting your child's period of night-time sleep either forwards (for late sleep phase) or backwards (for early sleep phase).

It is important that shifts are made gradually, so your child's body clock can accommodate the changes; if they are made too quickly, the plan is less likely to work. It is vital to stick rigidly to the new schedule, even at weekends and holidays, until you are certain that your child's body clock has fully adapted.

Before you embark on a sleep-phase plan, record a sleep diary (see pages 70–71) so you can work out when your child naturally falls asleep and wakes up.

Early sleep phase plan Early sleep phase is a sleep issue that mostly affects young children. To adjust it you simply delay your child's bedtime by an extra ten to 15 minutes every fourth day, until you arrive at your desired bedtime goal (see above). You may need to move mealtimes and daytime naps accordingly. During this period, do not interfere with your child's spontaneous wake times, which should naturally shift as his sleep onset time is moved. This programme can take a while and you need to make the adjustments slowly so that your child's body clock can catch up with your time changes. Bear in mind if you, or your family, naturally wake early, or are larks (see pages 18–19), your child may have inherited your chronotype and have a tendency to wake earlier than her contemporaries.

See also Solution 10 (pages 134–135) and Solution 17 (pages 148–149).

Late sleep phase plan This may be needed when a child's natural sleeping time shifts so that it is later than is typical for her age. Once she is asleep, she will sleep well and, if left to sleep on at weekends and holidays, will wake after a full night's sleep. However, if your child has to get up at a set time for nursery or school the chances are you will need to wake her. Getting washed, dressed and having breakfast can then be a challenge as she is often still sleepy and may be excessively tired in the day as a result of not having enough sleep.

Parents often regard late sleep phase as a bedtime battle or as an inability on the part of their child to fall asleep. An older child may become anxious about bedtime if she feels incapable of going to sleep.

This problem can arise:

- After holiday periods, when your child has become accustomed to being allowed to stay up later.

- When children do not have a set bedtime.

- If your child is anxious about bedtime.

- If your child has access to hand-held devices close to bedtime.

- In children who naturally have an owl chronotype (see pages 18–19).

- In children with ADHD (Attention deficit hyperactivity disorder) or with ASD (Autistic spectrum disorder), as they are more susceptible to delayed sleep phase.

Before you start on the sleep plan, explain to your child that she will be staying up a little later. However, it is best not to tell her what time that is.

Step 1

For the first three nights, aim to put your child to bed at the latest average time she naturally falls asleep. Start the bedtime routine only 30–40 minutes before putting her to bed. It is best not to mention bedtime until ten minutes beforehand and if she can tell the time, put away clocks so she does not inadvertently try to resist the plan.

Keep bedtime calm and relaxing and keep evening activities quiet. Do a puzzle together, read to her or do some colouring in; it is essential to avoid all screens for at least an hour before bed. Once you have said goodnight to her monitor how long she takes to fall asleep – it should be about 15 minutes. Just as importantly set her wake-up time based on when she has to get up for

Challenges of a late sleep phase plan

- For a short period at the start of this programme your child will be somewhat deprived of sleep and may be more irritable and tired on these days. However, if your child does not normally have a daytime nap it is best to avoid reintroducing one.

- Even if your child seems particularly tired, do not be tempted to rush and put her to bed much earlier than the plan, as the programme is less likely to work.

- As you approach your goal, your child may find it difficult to go to sleep at the desired time. If this happens, slow down the process and only move the time forward on a weekly basis.

- If your child is taking longer than 20 minutes to fall asleep, make her bedtime 15 minutes later the following night. Repeat this process until she is falling asleep well again, then start advancing bedtime again slowly.

See also Solution 18 (pages 150–151).

Introducing a late sleep phase plan

These guidelines are for a bedtime based on a child who normally falls asleep at 11.00pm. Take it slowly.

Steps	Start bedtime routine	Say goodnight	Asleep by	Waking time for every morning
Step one	10.15pm	10.45pm	11.00pm	7.15am
Step two	10.00pm	10.30pm	10.45pm	7.15am
Step three	9.45pm	10.15pm	10.30pm	7.15am
Step four	9.30pm	10.00pm	10.15pm	7.15am
Step five	9.15pm	9.45pm	10.00pm	7.15am
Step six	9.00pm	9.30pm	9.45pm	7.15am
Step seven	8.45pm	9.15pm	9.30pm	7.15am
Step eight	8.30pm	9.00pm	9.15pm	7.15am
Step nine	8.15pm	8.45pm	9.00pm	7.15am
Step ten	8.00pm	8.30pm	8.45pm	7.15am

nursery or school, and wake her at this time every morning regardless of what time she fell asleep at bedtime. Once she has achieved the bed – and wake-up time for three to four nights, proceed to the next step.

Step 2
Bring the bedtime routine and bedtime forward by 15 minutes, but keep the wake-up time the same. After another successful three to four nights advance bedtime by another 15 minutes, following the chart above. Be sure to record your child's sleep patterns on her sleep diary (see pages 70–71) so you can monitor her progress throughout.

Step 3
Repeat the process until you reach the bed- and wake-up times most appropriate for your child's needs (see pages 14–15) and her schedules. Then

the desired morning wake time should be firmly and consistently fixed every day – holidays and weekends included.

'Excuse me' plan timings	Nights	First check	Second check	Third and subsequent checks
	1	1 minute	2 minutes	3 minutes
	2	2 minutes	3 minutes	4 minutes
	3	3 minutes	4 minutes	5 minutes
	4	4 minutes	5 minutes	6 minutes
	5 and all subsequent nights	5 minutes	6 minutes	7 minutes

The 'excuse me' drill

If your child struggles to fall asleep without you or keeps calling for you, the 'Excuse me' drill is a gentle and responsive plan to help your child fall asleep independently. It works well for children aged three years and over who can cope when their parent leaves their bedroom for a few minutes, but ultimately want them to stay with them as they go to sleep. (See also Solution 9, pages 132–133).

What to do

- After your child's bedtime routine say goodnight, then briefly excuse yourself, for example say, 'you lie here nice and quietly, I just need to sort out the bathroom, I'll be back in a minute'. The excuse doesn't really matter – boring ones are best.

- Go back after a very short time, and when you return, briefly say 'Well done... you've been a very brave girl/boy to wait for me, night-night it's sleepy time'.

- Give your child a cuddle or kiss, make sure he is calm and settled and then give your next excuse and leave.

- Slowly increase the time you are out of your child's room, following the chart, above.

- If you feel you are progressing too quickly, repeat the same times for a few extra nights or reduce the minutes to seconds spent away.

- If your child gets up and follows you, calmly guide him back to bed, settle him and, when he is snuggled down, restart the drill. If he repeatedly becomes upset this may not be the right technique for your child – consider gradual retreat instead (see pages 72–74).

Scheduled stirring

This is a plan that can help with spontaneous night-wakers. This plan involves stirring your child around 15 to 30 minutes before his usual wake-up time so that he comes to a slightly higher level of sleep, but is not fully wake. How much you need to do to stir your child will vary from night to night. If he does wake, simply settle him back to sleep as you usually do.

Before you start, complete a sleep diary for a week so you know when your child wakes each night, and so when to 'stir' him. For example, if his first wake up time is 1.00am you would aim to stir him at 12.30am. If he wakes very easily move the stirring time 15 minutes earlier, say 12.15am.

- Start by saying his name.

- If this is not enough, then place a hand on him.

- If this is not enough, try to reposition him.

- Repeat this every night for a week.

- On week two stir him for six nights. For week three, stir him on five nights, leaving two consecutive nights of not stirring.

- Repeat the process, increasing the non-stirring nights, until you are no longer stirring him.

Responsive checking

This is a technique that should only be implemented under specific circumstances. It can be used for short-term sleep issues, such as after a holiday when your child's sleep has 'gone off track' for a week or two, or at the end of a gradual retreat plan when you have completed your steps but your child still needs you at the bedroom door to sleep. Your child should be more than eight months old and be happy to be left in his room for brief periods.

Initially it is best to implement it just at bedtime, when your child's sleep drive is high and melatonin levels will be good. Start with a relaxing bedtime routine to signal it is time for sleep. If your child can settle to sleep well and independently at bedtime, his night-time sleep will naturally improve after two to three weeks.

This plan involves putting your child down drowsy and then briefly leaving the bedroom. This could be for 30 seconds or a minute or two. On your return offer comfort, but then leaving again before he is fully asleep. The aim is to slowly extend the time you are out of the bedroom, but for no longer than five minutes. You decide how long to leave your child, based on his temperament and what you feel comfortable with. While you are out of the bedroom listen in to your child.

- If he is happily 'chatting' or just grizzling, wait to see if he is going to go to sleep.

- If he starts to cry or becomes upset, time your first check, then return to offer your child comfort and reassurance. This may mean a brief cuddle, stroke or pat, or an excuse such as 'I'll be back in a minute, I'm going to the bathroom'. It is important to leave again when your child is still awake.

- If he is standing in his cot, gently lay him down, offer a few strokes and leave again when he is calm.

- If he cries out again wait for another minute, then repeat your check.

- Continue to repeat your checks until your child quietens. At this point he is starting to settle himself to sleep and if you reappear now you are likely to interrupt it.

- If he is quiet for a few minutes, then starts to call out again, restart your checking as above, until he settles again.

Your child may take 30 to 40 minutes to go to sleep the first night, but this typically reduces considerably over the next three to four nights. If you have seen no real signs of improvement in your child's sleep over this period, consider using the gradual retreat plan instead (see pages 72–74).

Timings for responsive checking plan	You should decide how many seconds or minutes you feel comfortable to be out of your child's bedroom. Here is a guide:					
	First check	Second check	Third check	Fourth Check	Fifth check	Sixth and subsequent checks
	30 seconds	1 minute	2 minutes	3 minutes	4 minutes	5 minutes

Positive reinforcement – rewards

The parent who has never offered a reward as an incentive for changing their child's behaviour is a rare being. Most have also worried about crossing that fine line between positive reinforcement and downright bribery. However, if handled correctly, rewards can be beneficial and can work as well for sleep as for any other behavioural problem.

When and how to offer rewards

Rewards will only work if your child understands the concept inherent in reward-giving. This may sound obvious but many parents will, in understandable desperation, try to get their child to agree to a conditional behaviour before they are fully able to understand the concept of cause and effect. Your child also needs to be emotionally ready for deferred gratification because the reward or praise will not come until the following day.

Most children are able to understand these concepts by the age of three years. You will know if your child has reached this stage when she responds to conditional requests about other issues, such as tidy away the toys and we can read a book together, or only getting out another toy if she puts the first away.

What kind of reward?

Rewards fall into three categories: an object, such as a sticker, or something to collect; an activity, such as going on a picnic or an outing; and sensory or social rewards, such as hugs or special time with parents.

These can all work, and it is wrong to think that a durable object is more effective than, say, a cuddle with extra story time from you. Rewards that capture a child's imagination, such as the sleep

Man-made sunrise

Placing a 'magic' lamp in your child's room can work very well for early rising and some night-waking problems. The lamp is used with a timer switch and is set to come on at a given time. Using a low-wattage bulb will prevent the lamp waking your child unnecessarily. Finding the lamp on when she wakes will be her cue to get up, but if it is not on, she should return back to sleep. This approach works well with a reward system such as the sleep fairy (opposite).

Before using this method, establish your child's average waking times (see Keeping a sleep diary, pages 70–71). On the first day, set the lamp to come on 15 minutes before her 'normal' waking time, so that it is on when she wakes. Explain to your child that she must stay in bed until the lamp comes on and if she achieves this, the sleep fairy will leave a reward. Then slowly shift the time later every few days until the desired time is achieved. As your child moves closer to her target waking time, make changes weekly. If you try to force the time change too quickly you may jeopardize the progress you have already made. If your child cannot stay in bed until the lamp is on refer to see What if...?, page 89.

fairy (see below), or that emotionally stimulate her, such as warm praise, are as valuable to a child as an item from the toy shop.

Setting up and giving a reward

First, you need to know that the goal is achievable and the reward will be motivating for your child – you can talk to her about this. If you start with an easily achievable goal you will engage your child, and you can then gradually increase the requirements for receiving the reward.

You need to be very clear about the basic rules. Establish an understanding with your child about what she needs to achieve, as well as what the reward will be and when it will be given. It is worth remembering that a younger child's concept of time is still developing so she will be less able to wait; immediate rewards will be a greater incentive.

Once a reward has been given, never take is away, whatever your child's behaviour the day after, as it was given was for a very specific achievement. If your child begins to lose motivation revisit the reward system but make sure the goals are achievable and the reward is motivating for your child.

Practical rewards that work

The sleep fairy This is a fictional being who magically comes to the child's house when she is asleep at night and leaves her a reward. If your child does not respond to fairies, use a favourite story character instead.

Put the reward in a special little box or bag that sits next to your bed. This way, you, as the fairy's human agent, can put it in the box in the morning when you know your child merits it. Do not forget to play your part though. If your child has done well and goes to check her reward box and the fairy has not been, she may lose interest.

If a child's motivation wanes, or you need to stimulate her imagination, adding a written note from the fairy, or a picture or a little paper star from her wand, can all support the fantasy.

Star chart Rewarding children with a star tends to work well from about the age of four or five years, when they may have been exposed to the idea of stars as prizes at nursery or school. Make a chart and put a star on it for each day your child achieves the behaviour you have requested. Sometimes this alone, combined with verbal praise, is enough. If not, you can promise a small prize whenever your child has accumulated a certain number of stars. Instead of a chart, you could try marbles or pasta shapes in a jar as an incentive. However, do not make it too many or she may lose interest! If your child has a certain reward they would like to focus on, try printing off a picture of it and sticking it onto the chart or jar to motivate her.

Stopping the reward system

Most reward systems have a short shelf-life. But even if your child has reached the desired goal, it is best to continue rewards until her sleep pattern is well established.

Stopping the sleep fairy Make a point of not putting out a reward one night and when your child looks for it explain that the sleep fairy was visiting other children that night.

The 'fairy' can visit the following night, but gradually increase the number of nights when she is 'too busy' until you stop her visits completely. You could leave a note from the fairy on the final night saying 'Well done! Keep trying hard'.

Stopping the star chart Gradually 'forget' to offer stars. If your child reminds you, apologize for your bad memory and continue to offer stars for the next few nights before 'forgetting' again. Even though you stop offering stars, continue to praise and recognize your child's progress.

What if...?

While a well-planned and well-implemented programme has a very good chance of success, there are obviously sometimes glitches and setbacks on the way. Below are answers to some of the common 'What if...?' questions parents raise. Some of these are general, in that they can apply to many situations, others relate to particular circumstances or techniques described elsewhere in the book.

General problems

What if... my baby stands up in his cot?
This tends to happen towards the end of your baby's first year as he gains mobility and wants to practise his new-found skill. Problems arise if he cannot lower himself back down. Once resettled by you, he may get up again and it can become a game and a battle of wills that lasts until he falls asleep, exhausted.

Ensure your baby has plenty of floor time in the day. Teach him to lower himself from a standing position by practising pulling-up and sitting-back-down games.

When you are confident he can lower himself safely, leave him standing for short periods while you sit or lie by his cot. Occasionally tap the mattress and simply say 'It's sleepy time, lie down'. When he starts to tire, lay him down; if he springs straight up, ignore him and continue to lie low.

If he is happily standing and is content for you to leave him for a minute or two, you can come and go from the room, laying him down each time you return. You may have to repeat this numerous times, especially the first few nights. As soon as he stays lying down tell him he's a good boy and then settle him to sleep as you usually do.

What if... my baby rolls over in his sleep?
From around five to six months your baby will learn to roll. Once he is able to move from back to front and front to back again by himself, you can leave him to find his own sleeping position.

Until then, for safety reasons, you always need to put him in his cot in the 'back-to-sleep' position at bedtime (see Safe sleeping, pages 38–39) and if

Once your baby can stand in his cot, make sure he cannot harm himself if he falls.

he rolls onto his tummy, gently roll him onto his back again. Whatever you do, keep night-time interaction to a minimum. In the day, use lots of supervised floor-play to encourage rolling and help his natural development. A baby sleeping bag may help a restless baby.

What if… my baby loses his dummy?

If your baby is less than six months old and using a dummy, give it to him every time you put him down to sleep (day and night) for protection against SIDS (sudden infant death syndrome, see pages 38–39). If he spits it out while he is asleep, there is no need to keep putting it back. Between six and 12 months of age, you may wish to consider weaning your baby off his dummy.

You may be able to teach an older child to find and replace his own dummy, alternatively you can put extra dummies in the bed for him to find. It is even better to teach your child a new sleep association and to gradually wean him off a dummy altogether. Start this process by giving your child a dummy less and less often during the day, to reduce his dependency on it. Then, as you gain more confidence, do the same at night. To help achieve this, you may also need to use a sleep technique, such as gradual retreat (see pages 72–74).

What if… my toddler climbs out of his cot?

Start by lowering the mattress if you have not already done so. Remove objects such as teddy bears from his cot that he could climb on and gain leverage to push himself out. Do not inadvertently reward him for climbing out, for example, by taking him into your bed. Be calm and firm. Try to catch him early. Go into his room and firmly tell him not to climb out. If you do this consistently, he will probably get the idea and stay put.

If this fails, and your child repeatedly climbs out, it will be best to transfer him to a bed. You may also have to put a stair gate across his door to restrict night-time mobility and prevent accidents, and childproof his bedroom (see page 43).

What if… my child keeps asking for 'just one more'?

Many children are skilled in asking for 'just one more', whatever it is. Always give your child one chance – he may genuinely need help with his bedding, or a drink of water or a trip to the toilet.

Responding once will give him confidence that you are there if needed, after that, stay calm and be firm. Tell him 'it's time to sleep' and repeat this as necessary. You could encourage him to settle at bedtime by implementing a reward system (see pages 82–83) for laying quiet and still after you have said 'goodnight'.

What if… my child sneaks into our bed without us knowing?

Work out a way of alerting yourself whenever your child comes into the room. For example:

- Hang something such as a kitchen ladle or a fish slice onto the back of your door that will make a 'clang'.

- Put a wedge under your bedroom door, so that it is open but not enough for your child to get through without waking you.

- Put a stair gate across your bedroom door.

Take or send your child back to his bed every time he comes to your room – and remember to be consistent with this.

Illness
What… if my child is ill?

If your child is unwell you must do whatever is required to help him get better and consult your doctor if necessary. If you need to give medication, do so at the earliest opportunity to avoid discomfort or restless behaviour.

If your child will not settle at night, try to resist taking him into your bed. Instead, keep him in his own bed, but camp out in his room.

If you have stopped feeding your child at night, or are in the process of weaning him off night-feeds, you do not need to increase milk intake during the night. If he is dehydrated, it is better to offer water rather than milk first; his appetite will pick up as soon as he is well again.

Try to stall any sleep programmes until he is fully recovered, but protect the bedtime routine if possible. When you do restart, you may have three or four tricky nights until you see improvement again (see Times of change, Illness page 46).

What if... my baby is teething?
See Times of change, Teething, page 46.

Bedtimes
What if... my child doesn't want pre-bath milk?
If you have recently altered your child's bedtime routine to make milk the first element, rather than the last, it is likely to take her a few days to settle into this new routine. Try taking her to a quiet room, where there are no distractions, and calmly offering her the milk. Let her take her time – you can always offer the remainder as a top-up after her bath. Over the next few evenings she will gradually get used to having her feed before her bath and take more of it and become used to the new routine.

Make sure she eats well during the day. You can also try bringing her teatime forward a little if possible. She may then feel more like having the milk earlier.

What if... my partner would like to put our child to bed?
Are you in a pattern where it is always the same parent who puts your child to bed, but you now feel it is time to change? Your child may be used to one parent putting her to bed, and even insist on that parent, so you can rarely plan to go out in the evening. Your partner may want to be involved with that special cosy bedtime with your child.

There are times when it can be tricky to change things around, for example, you may be feeding your baby to sleep. When you are all ready to make the change, ensure your partner knows every detail of the bedtime routine, such as making sure your child has her last wee before she leaves the bathroom, not after she has settled in bed. You may want to start slowly by introducing your partner to elements of the process such the bath and the stories, then handing over to you for the last stage. Gradually work towards the point where your partner does it all. It is best to start when your evening diaries are clear so you be consistent over a number of days.

Try not to get involved if you can hear things taking longer than normal, or if your child starts calling for you, as this may undermine your partner's confidence and reinforce the suggestion that only you can do it 'properly'. You may find it easier to go for a walk or meet a friend.

What if... my child is anxious at bedtime and what can I do to help?
Anxiety is a natural response to a stressful event. It is part of the fight-or-flight mechanism essential for survival when we lived in the wild that, for example, helped us to run away from wild animals. In the modern world, we have very little need for this response, but our bodies still find it hard to differentiate between real or perceived danger. Being anxious at bedtime can trigger this stress response, and unsurprisingly, if your child's body thinks it is about to be chased by a tiger the last thing it will be able to do is sleep!

There are numerous causes of anxiety at bedtime and many can impact negatively on a child's sleep. These include long-term unresolved sleep issues, worrying about issues such as starting nursery or school, nightmares, fear of the dark and monsters, as well as family breakdowns and bereavements. The quiet of the night, when there are no distractions, is often the time worries or anxieties reappear.

A typical bedtime If a child is anxious she will usually struggle to fall asleep and can lie awake for hours. She may reappear numerous times in the evening with endless excuses about anything from being hungry, thirsty, too hot, too cold or needing the toilet. If you take her back to bed, she is back in no time with even more excuses. If this happens night after night it can lead to cross, stressed parents and an even more anxious child – you all dread bedtime! You may also find yourself having to get into your child's bed to help her sleep, then be woken in the night when she seeks you out again.

The good news is there are simple steps you can take to help your child settle to sleep well and take the stress out of bedtime. First, try to identify what might be causing your child to be anxious – this can go a long way towards solving the issue. Could it be something outside the home at nursery or school, such as friendship issues or the stress of starting a new school? Is it fear of the dark or monsters (see pages 132–133)?

If your child is anxious and distressed in the evening, reassure her and calmly and quietly take her back to her bed.

Or possibly a family issues such as a separation or bereavement? Has your child become fearful of sleep itself? We have seen this many times in children who have historically taken a long time to get to sleep. These children convince themselves they cannot sleep and become anxious as bedtime approaches.

Enjoy 'talking time' before bed It is best not to discuss your child's fears or worries at bedtime. Instead try to build in five to ten minutes of one-to-one time with her beforehand. Tidy away toys and, turn off the TV, put away the mobile phone and focus on each other. Use this special time to chat about the day, or what you are doing the next day. Ask your child if anything is worrying her. If your child does not want to chat now, try doing a quiet activity such as colouring in or a jigsaw together instead; she may talk then. Start the main bedtime routine when you have finished 'talking time'.

Handling gradual retreat
What if... my child keeps getting out of bed or talking or singing?
Before you start the plan take time in the day to fully explain to your child what will be happening at bedtime and overnight. Make sure she understands what you are going to do. Reassess your bedtime routine to ensure it is quiet and calming. And, if your child still has a nap, make sure it is not too long or too close to bedtime.

You can try using a reward system to encourage her to lie quietly in bed, while you sit on the sleep cushion or chair. If she is motivated, the reward will do the hard work for you.

If she still gets out of bed, stay calm and briefly remind her of the reward system. Do not fall into the trap of negotiating at this time of night – it is important to keep your sentences brief. If she doesn't mind you leaving the bedroom for a short period, go out for a few minutes and on your return remind her you will stay if she is quiet and in bed. You may need to repeat this a few times until he settles to sleep with you close by.

What if... my child takes a long time to go back to sleep even with a parent in the room?

Some children are kept awake by the presence of their parent in the room. You still need to retreat gradually every three to four days, but it may be that he will not go off to sleep quickly until you are finally outside the door.

What if... my child keeps waking up as I leave the bedroom?

Your child may not have entered into deep sleep before you left. Wait in the room for at least ten minutes after he has fallen asleep; for some children it takes a bit longer.

What if... my child becomes upset when I try sitting a little further away?

If may be best to slow down your progress and maintain your current position for a few extra nights before starting to move further away. Reassure him that you will stay with him until he is asleep. You may also wish to set up a reward system to encourage him as you move and to increase his motivation (see pages 82–83).

What if... I feel the whole process is taking too long?

As you are making gradual changes it can take up to six weeks to complete this type of sleep plan. Try to keep up the momentum, moving to the next stage every four to five nights. Importantly, you must not be tempted to rush this technique or it may not work.

Daytime napping

What if... I find it hard to get my baby to nap using the new settling technique in the daytime?

At the start of the programme, it is more important to establish the timing of your baby's naps rather than the detail of how he is going to sleep. Once your baby is settling well at bedtime, you can start to apply your chosen technique during the day too. You may find you have more success if you start by applying it to the first nap of the day, then move to the second and so on.

Handling sleep-phase problems

What if... my child has a late sleep phase, but I am reluctant to put him to bed later on a school night?

For this technique to be useful it is important to be consistent with your child's bed- and wake-up times (see pages 78–79). If you do not want a late bedtime on a school night it may be better to wait and start the plan in the school holidays.

What if... the bedtime is later, but my child is still taking a long time to go to sleep?

You may not have made it late enough, or may not be waking your child at the same time every morning. Keep a sleep diary while you are using the plan so you can see what time he falls sleep, and set that as the starting bedtime. Be consistent about waking him every day. Reassess your bedtime routine to ensure it is quiet and calm.

What if... my child wakes early but has had enough sleep?

There are children who go to sleep independently and stay asleep all night, but who are ready to face the world by 5.30am. They cope well with everyday routines and obviously do not need more sleep. If this is your child, teach him to stay in his bedroom reading or playing quietly until the rest of the family are ready to get up. Try setting up a timed lamp (see Man-made sunrise, page 82) or a digital clock if he is older, to indicate when it is alright to get out of bed. Try to set clear boundaries on what he is allowed to do in his room.

What if... my twins do not go to sleep at the same time?

If you have twins and would like them to sleep at the same time, establish set nap and bedtimes for them both. Create a simple routine that will suit both of them.

Be consistent about tucking them both up in bed at the same time. You may find one twin takes a little longer to fall asleep and that he needs some help, but as his sleep pattern becomes more established, gradually reduce this until he settles independently, too. Do not worry about one waking the other as most twins do not seem to be bothered by the other's sounds.

Revisit your bedtime routine if your child is taking a long time to go to sleep.

If your twins have very different sleep patterns, you can try resetting the body clock of the twin whose sleep times are causing you the most concern (see page 77).

What if... we are using the 'magic lamp' system, but my child cannot stay in bed until the lamp comes on?
You may have set the timer for too late and the time between him waking and the light coming on is too long. Reset it so the lamp comes on just after your child wakes naturally and use a reward system to motivate him to stay in bed. Once he is happily onboard and able to wait in his bed, gradually move the timer later, but by only five to 15 minutes at a time.

Using rewards
What if... my child does not respond to rewards?
Try offering a different reward. If using the sleep-fairy/story character method, 'deliver' an extra fairy note as an extra boost (see page 83). Above all, keep the concept alive. Also, your child may conveniently forget the reward system if he thinks the task expected of him is too difficult, so re-evaluate the goals you have set him to ensure they are achievable.

You can adapt the rewards and communication with the fairy endlessly to increase your child's motivation.

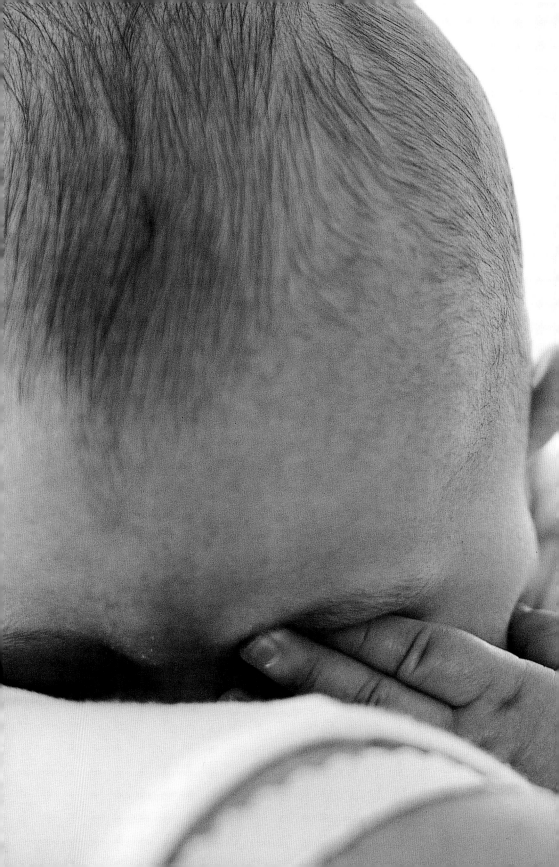

Identifying the problem

How to use our flow charts

We have designed a series of flow charts to help you identify the nature of your child's sleep issue. They then direct you to more detailed supporting information in the heart of the book. This may be in the form of background information on sleep, technical descriptions, developmental stages, and/or solutions, or case studies, from families we have worked with.

Each flow chart looks at a common sleep dilemma and takes you through a series of questions, exploring specific aspects of the issue, to help to identify an appropriate plan. This exploration mirrors the type of questions we use at Millpond Children's Sleep Clinic when we are seeking to define the exact nature of the difficulties being experienced by our families. You will see that in several instances we have looked at the same issue for a range of age groups, as the underlying reasons may differ according to your child's age.

Using the flow charts is simple: first identify the issue that most closely matches your own, then follow the questions and suggestions it contains. As many families know, sleep problems often come in multiples, so you may find that more than one flow chart applies to you.

Any plan you adopt will work best if it is tailored to your child's sleep problem. Your child's age, his personality and circumstances, as well as your domestic arrangements and your own parenting style can all play a part in your decision as to what best suits you both (see also Chapter 4, Addressing sleep concerns, pages 66–89).

Choose a plan you feel you can stick to – ensuring you have realistic expectations for yourself and your child will help you achieve the results you are aiming for. When it comes to implementing it, try to remain consistent and repetitive. We advise parents to keep a sleep diary (see pages 70–71) – an essential tool that will not only help you track your progress, but also flag up areas where you might need to make adjustments.

A child's sleep needs and routine will change a number of times from baby to child.

Flow chart 1 How can I manage daytime napping?

Good daytime naps are the foundation of a good night's sleep. Daytime sleep can impact on night-time sleep in many ways. A child who sleeps well in the day tends to sleep better and more predictably at night. While a baby who takes very short, frequent naps, has too much or too little sleep, or who naps at the 'wrong' time in the day, may well have issues with his night-time sleep.

The solution is not to restrict your child's naps in the hope that he will compensate by sleeping longer at night. Instead, focus on the when and how much sleep he has in the day, and ensure that it is correct for his age.

What kind of napping schedule should my baby follow?

Your baby's napping schedule will change with age but, as a general rule, the older your child, the less sleep he needs in the day.

See pages 20–25, Developmental stages and sleep

See page 34, Number and length of naps

Do you know when your baby is tired?
Learning to recognize your baby's sleep cues will help to prevent overtiredness in the day.

See pages 28, The sleep cues

Do you have difficulties getting your baby to sleep during the day?

Do you have a structure to your child's naps?
It helps if regular nap times are spaced evenly throughout the day. Plan them for after meals so that your child does not fall asleep hungry and wake too soon. Implement a routine, similar to the bedtime one but shorter, before each nap so that your child is calm, relaxed and ready for sleep.

See pages 32–35, Naps

See pages 116–117, Solution 1

Will your child only settle in the car or buggy for daytime naps?

If you want your child to have at least one of his naps in his cot, start by creating a nap schedule. Once regular nap times are established and his night-time sleep is settled, you can start to teach him how to settle in his cot in the day.

See pages 72–81, Sleep strategies

See pages 32–35, Naps

See page 53, Inappropriate sleep-onset associations

Does your child have a very late nap, then find it difficult to settle at bedtime?

If you have problems settling your child in the evening and he is napping late in the afternoon, his nap is probably too close to bedtime. Consider bringing the afternoon nap forward gradually until he sleeps well at bedtime. You may need to adjust your child's mealtimes and other naps to accommodate this change.

See page 32, Spacing – the key to good naps

See page 34, Number and length of naps

See pages 116–117, Solution 1

Does your child take only very short naps?

Young babies have short nap cycles, but between three and 12 months the cycle lengthens. If your child repeatedly wakes too soon, he may become overtired; catnaps only take the edge off tiredness. This sporadic sleeping could be repeated at night.

See page 35, Napping problems

See page 32, Spacing – the key to good naps

A ten to 15 minute pre-nap routine will help your child to establish regular napping.

Flow chart 2 How can I get my baby to sleep (birth to six months)?

The first few weeks with your new baby will go by in a blur of feeding, nappy changing and sleeping. Your newborn baby sleeps just as much in the day as the night, but there is seemingly no pattern. But as you gain confidence and get to grips with your baby's habits, you may decide now is the time to consider introducing a simple bedtime routine for your baby to help him to establish good sleep habits.

Have you started introducing a bedtime routine for your baby?

Evidence shows that it is best to start implementing a simple, predictable bedtime routine for your baby in the first few weeks, so she starts to understand that having quiet and winding-down time in the evening means it is nearly time to sleep.

See page 20,
Developmental stages
and sleep, Birth to
six months

See pages 28–29,
Helping your
young baby into a
good sleep rhythm

See pages 30–31,
Creating
a sleep routine

Tuning into your baby's sleep cues will help her to settle more easily.

See pages 28–29,
Helping your
young baby into a
good sleep rhythm

Could your baby could be overtired?
Tuning into your baby's sleep cues helps
you recognize when she is tired and
you can put her down to nap or to bed,
to prevent her becoming overtired.

See page 28,
The sleep cues

See page 20,
Developmental
stages and sleep,
Birth to six
months

**Is your baby having enough naps,
or too much sleep in the day?**
A baby who is overtired or not tired
enough at bedtime will find it hard
to fall asleep.

See page 34,
Number and
length of naps

**Does your
baby cry a lot
when you try
to settle her to
sleep?**

Is your baby over-stimulated?
If your baby becomes over-
stimulated she is likely to be
harder to settle to sleep.

See pages 28–29,
Helping your
young baby into
a good sleep
rhythms

**Could your baby be suffering
from the symptoms of colic?**
Characterized by long periods of
inconsolable crying that starts and
stops without obvious cause, colic can
disrupt day- and night-time sleep.

See pages 58–59,
Infant colic

**Could your baby could be suffering
from the symptoms of reflux?**
Reflux can create stomach pains rather like
heartburn, which are more uncomfortable
when your infant is lying down, making it
harder for her to fall asleep.

See page 59,
Gastro-
oesophageal
reflux

Flow chart 3 How can I get my child to sleep (six months to toddler)?

Once your baby reaches six months, his sleeping and waking will be more organized and he has the ability to sleep for longer periods at night. However, he is about to go through some rapid developmental changes and challenges that could test your well-established bedtime routine. That young baby who used to fall peacefully sleep within minutes, has suddenly become an older baby or toddler who resists bedtime and who does not want you to leave him.

Do you have to pat, rock or hold your child before he goes to sleep?

It is common for children of this age to rely on sleep props at bedtime, which can be anything from wanting you to rock him to only falling asleep in your bed. Aim to establish a bedtime routine that helps your child fall asleep independently, encouraging a better night's sleep. You may want to consider a sleep strategy.

See pages 30–31, Creating a sleep routine

See page 53, Inappropriate sleep-onset associations

See pages 72–74, Gradual retreat plan

Does your child stand up as soon as you put him in the cot?

If your child is happy and thinks this is a game, sit low beside his cot, and every few minutes gently lie him down again until he eventually stays down and goes to sleep. If he cannot lie down from standing offer lots of floor play in the daytime so that he can practice his skills.

See page 84, What if... my baby stands in his cot?

**Does your child nap late
in the afternoon?**
Your child's last nap may be too close
to bedtime.

See pages 32–35,
Naps

See pages 30–31,
Creating a sleep
routine

Do you have a regular time for bed?
A simple, predictable bedtime routine that
is at the same time every day helps a child
to learn when it is time to sleep.

See pages 30–31,
Creating a sleep
routine

**Does your child
take a long time
to fall asleep?**

Is your child overtired?
Children who are overtired can find
it difficult to settle and take longer to
go to sleep.

See pages 32–35,
Naps
See pages 14–15,
What to expect of
your child's sleep
See pages 118–119,
Solution 2

**Is your bedtime routine effective at winding
your child down?**
If your child remains over-stimulated and
excited he will struggle to settle himself.

See pages 30–31,
Creating a sleep
routine

**Does your child appear to be overtired
at bedtime?**
If your child's naps are irregular or too short
this could lead him being overtired and so to a
fractious bedtime.

See pages 32–35,
Naps
See pages 30–31,
Creating a sleep
routine

**Does your
child cry as
soon as you
place him in
the cot?**

**Has your child suddenly started to cry when
you leave the bedroom? Does this happen
during play in the daytime too?**
At between seven and nine months of age
babies start to exhibit separation anxiety.
This is normal developmental stage but it
can affect sleep too.

See pages 20–25,
Developmental
stages and sleep

See pages 72–74,
Gradual retreat
plan

**Could your child be experiencing pain
or discomfort?**
Being unwell or in discomfort from
teething, for example, can affect your
child's ability to settle.

See pages 42–43,
Times of change
See pages 58–63,
Other problems
affecting sleep
See page 46,
Teething

Flow chart 4 How can I get my child to sleep (toddler to six year old)?

This is the time when your child is gradually becoming more independent, aware of her world, the control she has over it, and her place within it. She will be busy learning, creating, running, climbing and experiencing new places outside the home such as nursery and school. And with so much going on in her life, it is not surprising that her sleep can be affected by it.

Does your child resist going to bed? Does she come up with endless excuses and requests, or keep coming to or calling for you after bedtime?

Many children of this age find it hard to switch off their busy brains at bedtime, or they want to test your boundaries – can they talk you into another story/kiss/drink… Assess your bedtime routine – is it quiet, calm and relaxing enough to help her wind down. And do you start at the same time every night. Try setting aside ten minutes after her supper to discuss her day, rather than chatting things through at bedtime. Set limits you can keep to – when you say just one more story, make sure it is. A reward system focused on bedtime behaviour works wonders.

See pages 30–31,
Creating a sleep routine

See pages 82–83,
Positive reinforcements – rewards

See pages 72–81,
Sleep strategies

See pages 124–125,
Solution 5

Do you have to stay with your child while she goes off to sleep?

She may have developed inappropriate sleep-onset associations. If you need to stay with her at bedtime this could result in night-time waking too, when she is likely to seek your help again to get back to sleep.

See page 53,
Inappropriate sleep-onset associations

See pages 120–121,
Solution 3

Does your child have a late nap or is still napping when she no longer needs to?

Your child may not be tired enough to go to sleep at an appropriate bedtime. If she still has an afternoon nap try bringing it forward, or even dropping it.

See pages 32–35,
Naps

Is your child anxious or frightened at bedtime?

As children's imaginations develop and they gain more independence outside the home, it is not uncommon for them to experience fears and/or anxieties. These emotions often manifest at bedtime, and can be the root cause of her having difficulty falling asleep.

See pages 20–25,
Developmental stages and sleep

See page 86,
What if... my child is anxious at bedtime?

See pages 122–123,
Solution 4

Start quiet time an hour before bedtime so that your child will be ready to fall asleep.

Flow chart 5 My baby is waking in the night (six months to toddler)

Your baby's sleeping and waking patterns become more organized from the age of about six months and he can sleep for longer periods at night (see What to expect of your child's sleep, pages 14–15). But evidence shows that night-waking is common until 12 months old and only then will he sleep more predictably all night.

All children wake briefly numerous times as they pass through different stages of sleep (see Sleep cycles, pages 16–17); those who can settle themselves to sleep independently will also do so at night without needing to wake their parents. Children who need help to return to sleep after night-waking is one of the most common sleep difficulties for parents – around 25 to 50 per cent of babies and toddlers wake frequently at night.

Are you sure your child is fully awake?

Sometimes you may think your child is waking when he is in fact just in a phase of light sleep. He may partially wake naturally, call out, then drift back to sleep if left undisturbed.

See pages 16–17, Sleep cycles

Has your baby started to cry when you leave the room both in the day and at bedtime as well as wake and cry out for you in the night?

If your baby is around seven to nine months old he may be experiencing separation anxiety. This normal stage of development means your baby has reached the stage where he knows you are leaving, but is not yet sure that you will return. If he wakes at night he is likely to call out to be reassured that you are there. But check too if he is teething or is unwell.

See pages 20–25, Developmental stages and sleep

See page 46, Times of change, Illness

See pages 58–63, Other problems affecting sleep

Does your child want a feed when he wakes?
It is normal for babies under a year to wake at
night for feeds, but this is not always the cause
of night waking. You may need to consider
other reasons why your child is waking.

See pages 144–147,
Solutions 15
and 16

See pages 30–31,
Creating a sleep
routine

See page 53,
Inappropriate sleep-
onset associations

See pages 72–74,
Gradual retreat plan

*See pages 118–119,
128–129 and 140–141,*
Solutions 2, 7 and 13

**Does your baby or toddler need rocking or
cuddling during the night to get to sleep?**
Your child may have inappropriate sleep-onset
associations. Consider how he falls asleep.
Research shows if your child learns to fall
asleep independently at bedtime, in a few
weeks he will be able to do it at night too. Using
a gentle sleep plan will help him learn how to
self-settle at bedtime, enabling him to resettle
himself during the night.

**Why might
my older
baby/toddler
be waking?**

Could your child be in pain or unwell?
Your child could be teething or be constipated?
Does your child have reflux or allergies? Check
his temperature and look for other signs of
illness. These can all disrupt sleep. If you
suspect your child is unwell, seek medical advice
as soon as possible.

See page 46,
Times of change,
Illness

See pages 58–63,
Other problems
affecting sleep

Is he going through a developmental leap?
If your child is in the process of learning a new motor skill, for example,
crawling, and is otherwise fit and well, this could be the cause of his
sleep disruption. The onset of developmental leaps can result in a
temporary increase in wakeful episodes at night. Help him through this
stage by ensuring he is getting the right amount of sleep for his age and
aim to keep to your regular bedtime routine.

Do you think your child is too hot or cold?
Your baby's room temperature should be 16-20°C (60–68°F). Feel the back
of his neck or chest to see if he is too hot or too cold – hands and feet can
feel cooler even when your child is perfectly warm. Remove or add a layer
of bedding if necessary.

Flow chart 6 My child is waking at night (toddler to six year old)

Night-waking is one of the most common sleep difficulties faced by parents. Studies show night waking occurs in 25 to 50 per cent of children. There are many reasons why young children wake, but the most common cause is inappropriate sleep-onset associations – in other words, how your child falls asleep, what she associates with sleep and her ability to return back to sleep independently when she stirs into light sleep.

There are a number of strategies parents can use to help their child sleep well, with strong evidence to support behavioural modification being the most effective. It is important to nip the problem in the bud as sleep problems that present in infancy may persist into the pre-school and school-age years. And, the sooner your address night waking, the easier it will be to resolve.

Do you have to provide certain conditions in the night for your child to go back to sleep?

If your child needs you lay or sit with her when she goes to sleep at bedtime and you have to provide the same conditions when she wakes in the night she may have acquired inappropriate sleep-onset associations.

See page 53, Inappropriate sleep-onset associations

See pages 72–81, Sleep strategies

See pages 120–121, 128–129, 130–131, 142–143, 144–145 and 154–155, Solutions 3, 7, 8, 14, 15 and 20

Have you recently transferred your child from a cot to a bed?
Moving from a cot to a bed can provide your child with a new-found freedom. Until your child is motivated to stay in their bed all night the problem may persist. If your child needs you at night to help her get back to sleep, she will physically seek you out.

See pages 72–81, Sleep strategies

See pages 124–125, 130–131 and 138–139, Solutions 5, 8 and 12

Does your child keep calling out for you or coming to find you in the night?

See page 37, Fear of the dark

Does your child wake and appear frightened or anxious?
Your child could be experiencing a fear of the dark, night terror a nightmare.

See pages 55–57, Nightmares and night terrors

See pages 132–133 and 152–153, Solutions 9 and 19

Does your older child wake because she has wet the bed?

See pages 62–63, Bed-wetting

Moving your child from a cot to a bed can be the start of night waking episodes.

Flow chart 7 Weaning from night feeds (older baby to child)

You may want to wean your baby from her night feeds because you feel the time is right. Or she is nearly one year old and you are about to return to work and are worried how you will cope with a job and the sleep disruption of numerous night feeds.

Before you make any changes ensure she is growing well, reaching her developmental milestones, and eating and drinking happily during the day as expected for her age. You do not have to stop all night feeds; you may prefer to just reduce the number. Whatever you decide it is best to manage this process slowly and consistently.

It is common and usual for babies under a year to wake for night feeds.

Are you unsure how to reduce or wean your baby's night feeds?

Is your child having two or three large feeds a night?

It is best to wean your child by slowly reducing the volume of the chosen feed; if bottle-feeding, decrease the milk by 10ml ($\frac{1}{3}$fl oz) per night; for breastfeeding reduce the length of the feed by one minute every few nights. If you wish to keep one feed, choose a time that suits you both, such as 3.00am, and offer her that feed as usual, but continue to reduce the others.

See pages 74–76, Reducing night-time feeds for a baby over six months old

See pages 144–145, Solution 15

Does your child have short, frequent feeds and generally settle immediately?

If your child settles on the breast or bottle at bedtime, and falls asleep quickly when offered feeds at night, having taken a small amount, she may have developed inappropriate sleep-onset associations. You may find it best to start weaning from night feeds by spacing first. At bedtime try a gentle sleep plan to encourage her to fall asleep.

See pages 30–31, Creating a sleep routine

See page 53, Inappropriate sleep-onset associations

See page 75, Sleep strategies, spacing frequent night-time feeds

See pages 142–143, Solution 14

Are you concerned how to settle your baby at night without feeding him?

Once you have reduced, or weaned your baby off, her night feeds it is time to encourage her to settle independently. Initially you may like to start this process just at bedtime, then once she has adapted well to this, apply the same strategy if she wakes in the night.

See pages 30–31, Creating a sleep routine

See pages 36–37, Creating the right environment

See page 53, Inappropriate sleep-onset associations

See pages 72–81, Sleep strategies

See pages 118–119 and 140–147, Solutions 2, 13, 14, 15, and 16

Flow chart 8 My child wakes up very early

Early morning waking is one of the most exhausting problems for parents and because their child's sleep drive is very low at this time of day it is also one of the most difficult to solve. Your child's early rising can be the result of hunger, excessive daytime naps, an exceptionally early bedtime or inadvertently encouraged rewards, such as watching the television or a tablet. It may also be due to environmental factors. However, some children are natural larks (see pages 18–19), while others simply need less sleep.

Is your child sensitive to environmental factors?

Check whether your child's room is too light in the morning, too warm or too cold (it should be 16-20°C/60–68°F). Is there excessive noise inside or outside your home?

See pages 36–37, Creating the right environment for sleep

See pages 14–15, What to expect of your child's sleep

Early waking can occur if your baby or child is napping for too long during the day, as he may take this sleep from his night-time sleep quota. It may be best to reduce his naps.

See pages 32–35, Naps

See pages 20–25, Developmental stages and sleep

Could your child be sleeping too much in the daytime?

Is your baby ready to nap within an hour of getting up?
If he needs to sleep so soon after getting up it suggests that this early morning nap is an extension of his night-time sleep. You will need to gradually to move this nap later – aim for it to take place two to three hours after he first wakes.

See page 32, Spacing – the key to good naps

Does your child fall asleep in the early evening, sleep through the night but wake very early in the morning?

Your child's natural night-time sleep period is starting too early within the 24-hour day. You will need to gradually delay bedtime until his sleep period has shifted to an appropriate time.

See pages 14–15, What to expect of your child's sleep?

See page 77, Resetting your child's body clock

Does your older baby wake for an early morning feed?
Is your baby over six months old and waking for a morning feed around 5.00am, then struggling to go back to sleep? If your baby is well, thriving and eating solids, you can gently and gradually shift this early morning feed forward to after 6.00am.

See page 75, Spacing frequent night-time feeds

See pages 148–149, Solution 17

Are you inadvertently encouraging early rising by 'rewarding' your child's behaviour?
If your child has an incentive to wake early, for example because he has been told he can watch TV or play with toys if he is quiet, it is likely this has become a learned behaviour. To stop this habit, remove the incentives and encourage your child to stay in his bed until it is time to get up; a reward system can work wonders.

See pages 82–83, Positive reinforcement – rewards (especially Man-made sunrise)

See pages 150–151, Solution 18

Does your child seem to need less sleep than other children?
Some children really do need less sleep. These children wake early but appear rested and happy, and cope well with daily routines.

See pages 14–15, What to expect of your child's sleep?

See pages 88–89, What if...?, Handling sleep-phase problems

Flow chart 9 My child settles very late

Your child may be unable to fall asleep until well after the desired bedtime, which often results in stressful bedtime for all. Once asleep your child may sleep well and, if left, wakes late in the morning. However, she has to be woken to start daily routines and is often tired in the day. Her natural sleep period has shifted and starts too late, creating what is known as a 'late sleep phase'. This can affect children of all ages and often arises after holidays and illnesses or if your child is anxious or has an irregular bedtime. It is more common if your child has an owl-type chronotype (see page 19).

Has your child's natural sleep period shifted so it starts and finishes late?

Do you have problems getting your child to sleep at bedtime and waking her in the morning?

If your child has a late sleep phase, she may not be having enough sleep. Keep a sleep diary for a week to work out what time she naturally falls asleep. Then move your relaxing bedtime routine to her natural sleep time, however late that is. When she has learned how to fall asleep well at this 'new' time, you can gradually shift her body clock back. Taking her into the light as soon as possible in the morning will also help.

See pages 14–15,
What to expect of your child's sleep?

See pages 70–71,
Keeping a sleep diary

See pages 78–79,
Resetting your child's body clock, Late sleep phase plan

See pages 150–151,
Solution 18

Do you struggle to get your child to bed at 'bedtime'?

Your expectations for bedtime may be earlier than the time your child is naturally ready to sleep, resulting in stress and fuss. Start by checking how much sleep she needs for her age – she may be having enough. If she is struggling with lack of sleep, you can gradually move her body clock with the late sleep phase plan.

See page 14,
Average sleep needs in childhood

See pages 70–71,
Keeping a sleep diary

See pages 78–79,
Resetting your child's body clock, Late sleep phase plan

See pages 150–151,
Solution 18

Flow chart 10 Nightmares and night terrors

Nightmares and night terrors are quite different phenomena (see pages 55–57). Nightmares are frightening dreams that wake a child and require reassurance from parents. They are a normal part of development and are most common in children aged between three and ten years.

Fewer children experience night terrors, which are related to sleep-walking and sleep-talking. Most children who have these have outgrown them by puberty. Night terrors can be distressing for parents to watch, but in fact the child is deeply asleep and totally unaware of what is happening.

Does your child 'wake' in the first third of the night, confused and crying out?

Does your child appear frightened, cry out or scream and become hot and sweaty?
If your child has a 'glassy look', with her eyes wide open, apparently does not know you are there, she is probably having a night terror. She will not respond to you and, after a few minutes, she will go back to sleep and is unlikely to remember the episode in the morning.

See page 56, Sleep disorders and parasomnias, night terrors

See pages 152–153, Solution 19

Does your child wake, afraid and crying, more commonly in the early hours of the morning?

Your child has most probably had a nightmare. Children remember nightmares and, if old enough, can describe them to you. Your child will be fully alert when she is awake and will recognize you. She will need comfort and reassurance to feel safe and secure, but as she will still be tired she is likely to go back to sleep after a few minutes.

See page 56, Sleep disorders and parasomnias, nightmares

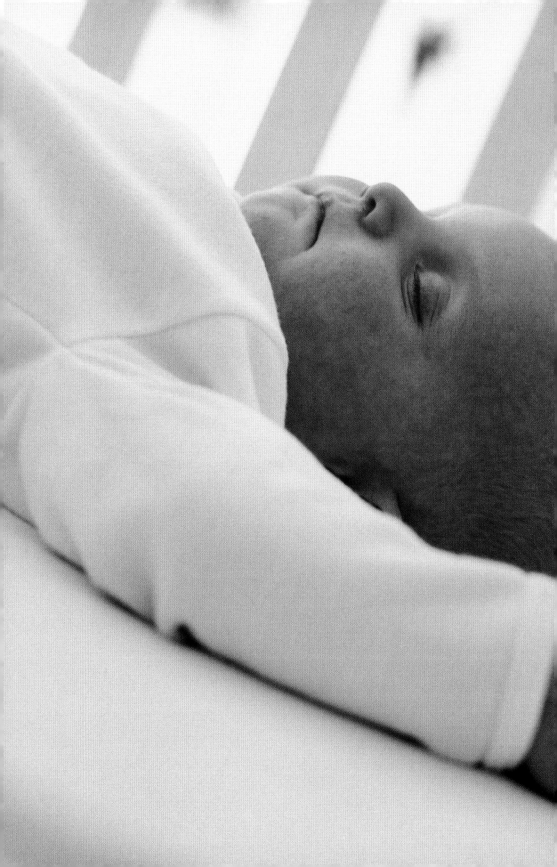

Sleep
solutions

How to use the solutions

This chapter includes a series of genuine case studies that we have dealt with at Millpond Children's Sleep Clinic. Chosen to represent the range of techniques that can be used to address sleep issues, they illustrate how families whose children have been experiencing sleep problems have worked to overcome those problems.

You will find the flow charts in Chapter 5, and the techniques outlined in Chapter 4 will direct you to these numbered 'Solutions'. In this way you can see how parents have successfully treated real-life sleep problems by following the clearly defined techniques outlined in this book.

Each solution is set out in the same way. Firstly, there is a detailed description of the background, which explains how the problem manifested itself and its impact on the child and the family. Next we present our thoughts, or analysis, of the key issues that need to be looked at. This leads on to the plan, which takes into account the family circumstances and outlines the best strategy for dealing with the key problem in that particular situation. We then present the 'result': a brief examination of what happened when the plan was implemented.

Finally, the individual steps of the plan are set out on the right-hand page to give you practical guidance on how you can apply this problem at home. Your situation is unlikely to match the case and family circumstances outlined exactly, but we hope you will be able to draw lessons – and encouragement – from what you read.

Find the problem that most closely matches yours and then apply the solution. You should begin to see how the techniques and principles outlined in the book can be applied to a whole range of problems in a wide variety of circumstances. You will find that consistency and time will bring their reward. When applying most sleep programmes, you may find the first night of each stage is the hardest, the second night is better, but the third night can be slightly harder again. Persevere, and once you get past the third night test your child's sleep should start to settle.

If you are starting to read this book by referring to the solutions described here, you will find pointers to the earlier chapters where aspects of sleep and our sleep plans are explained in more detail. Carefully applied, the plans should bring you the same success – and welcome rest.

Only start your sleep plan when you can be fully committed.

Solution 1 I'm really struggling with my older baby's naps

Try this plan if, like Rosie, your older baby only has short naps and seems tried and grumpy in the day.

Background

Rosie was nine months old, with a two and a half year old brother Tom. She usually woke early in the morning at about 5.30am and had frequent short naps throughout the day.

Rosie very rarely woke happily from her naps and was often fractious and tearful during the day. Mum had tried settling Rosie back to sleep when she woke too early from her naps, but she was very resistant to this and rarely resettled. It upset mum to see that Rosie spent most of her day tried and grumpy. She was also concerned that as Rosie woke too early in the morning she was generally not getting enough sleep.

In addition, as Rosie's naps were short, it meant that mum had very little time to do anything with Tom. Rosie also woke very easily from her naps – the slightest noise seemed to disturb her. As a result mum was always trying to keep Tom quiet when Rosie napped, but there were still times when the sound of his playing woke her.

A typical day for Rosie:

5.30am – Wake up	2.30pm – 30-minutes nap
8.00am – 30-minute nap	5.30pm – 30-minutes nap
11.30am – 45-minute nap	8.00pm – Asleep for the night

Our view

The fact that Rosie was grumpy and unhappy when she woke from her short naps suggested she was still tired and in need of more sleep. She wanted her first nap by 8.00am because she usually woke so early in the morning, but having an early morning nap can contribute to early rising. Rosie seemed sensitive to background noise, which meant the whole family had to creep about when she was asleep.

Sleep plan

The plan was to gradually increase the time between Rosie's naps and to encourage her to have fewer, longer naps, which would also help with the early rising. This would be done slowly by keeping her awake for an additional 10 minutes each day, until she was down to two naps, a 45-minute morning one starting at about 10.00am, and a 90-minute afternoon nap starting at about 2.00pm. Tom had his afternoon nap at 1.30pm. Mum wanted one of Rosie's naps to be in the buggy so that she had the flexibility to go out with Tom and she decided the morning nap would be best for this.

Mum introduced pre-nap wind down to prepare Rosie for her naps. In a similar way to bedtime, she had ten minutes of quiet time – a cuddle and a story – then took Rosie into the bedroom and closed the curtains. A darkened room for her naps would prevent her from becoming distracted by things in the room. The goal was to settle Rosie into her cot in the same way she did at bedtime.

To help Rosie sleep longer for her afternoon nap, mum was to use scheduled stirring (pages 80–81). She would pre-empt her waking by going to the cot after she had been asleep for 30 minutes. When she saw signs of Rosie coming into lighter, more active sleep, mum was to stroke or pat her back to sleep. If this was very difficult, mum was to use the buggy for two weeks for both naps to establish a sleep pattern. Once it was set, then she could then settle Rosie in her cot again.

Mum would use white noise for the home naps to try and prevent Rosie being disturbed by background sounds.

Results

Mum found it easy to keep Rosie awake for increasingly longer periods during the day using toys and stories to distract her. However, as expected, mum struggled to resettle Rosie in her cot in the afternoons. She decided to use the buggy for the first two weeks to establish the routine. The lack of sleep hormones in the day means nap problems usually take longer to settle than night-time sleep issues.

By the end of week three mum had established two naps for Rosie and her afternoon one usually lasted one and half to two hours. Rosie was now waking closer to 7.00am most mornings.

Rosie had some naps in the buggy and some in her cot and mum liked this flexibility. Occasionally there were days when it was harder to get her back to sleep in her cot in the afternoon, so mum rocked her. Playing the white noise during her naps meant Rosie was no longer woken by Tom playing.

Having a ten-minute quiet wind down with your baby prior to her nap will help her settle well and nap longer.

Steps

Step 1 Keep a record of your baby's usual nap schedule in a sleep diary (see pages 70–71) for a week so you can see what times they usually occur.

Step 2 Check the napping guide on pages 32–35 to see which schedule is suitable for your baby's age.

Step 3 Increase the time between your baby's naps by just ten minutes a day until they are spaced further apart and longer.

Step 4 Prepare your baby for her nap with ten minutes of quiet time – tidy away toys and sit with her looking at a book or having a cuddle. Look out for her sleep cues (see page 28) as it is a combination of nap timing and sleep cues that gets the best results.

Step 5 To help your baby link two sleep cycles together, when she has been asleep for 30 minutes, gently pat, stroke and/or shush her until she is fully asleep again. As naps usually take longer to settle than night-time sleep issues, you will need to persevere longer – do not just give up after a day or two.

Step 6 It is best to spend a couple of weeks establishing your baby's napping schedule first, then decide which plan you would like to use to help settle her (see Sleep strategies, pages 72–81).

Solution 2 How can I settle my baby or toddler to sleep?

Try this plan if, like Zane, your baby has erratic, inconsistent bedtimes, irregular naps and no pattern to his sleep.

Background

Zane was nine months old and an only child. From his first months he resisted being put in his cot for his naps and at bedtime and would only sleep if he was rocked until deeply asleep, then put in his cot.

Quote from mum
'Zane's dad and I spend very little time together. We would like to establish a regular bedtime for Zane as we can see the impact sleep deprivation is having on his behaviour and mood.'

Zane's day was erratic, with no regular meal or nap times. His naps consisted of two 30-minute sessions – much less than the two or more hours appropriate for his age; some days he hardly slept. His bedtime varied from 7.00 to 9.00pm. He needed to be held and carried most of the day; he found it hard to focus and play.

On a typical evening he was fed around 6.30pm, given a bath at 7.00pm, by which time he was usually overtired and fractious, and needed to be rocked to sleep. He would be put in his cot at 7.30pm – very carefully to prevent him waking. However, he usually woke up crying as soon as he was put down. His parents would pick him up and try rocking and walking with him again and again – it often took an hour or more to get him to sleep. Some evenings, out of exhaustion, his parents took him into the living room until he fell deeply asleep, then placed him in his cot. They even resorted to taking him out in the buggy late at night.

This pattern continued all night, every night, as Zane woke up four or five times. He needed a feed once or twice, but mostly he just wanted to be rocked back to sleep. After such unsettled nights, Zane's day started anywhere between 7.00 and 9.00am.

Our view

Zane had no structure to his day- or night-time sleep. He was chronically overtired, so was easily over-stimulated, which made it difficult for him to settle to sleep. He had no set sleep routine or regular bedtime, and associated being rocked by his parents or in his buggy with sleep. He eventually fell asleep out of sheer exhaustion. The knock-on effect was that his day often started late, which disrupted daytime sleep patterns. Zane was unable to settle by himself at bedtime or when he woke at night.

Sleep plan

To regulate Zane's body clock, it was essential to have a set bedtime routine and time, and just as importantly a set wake-up time. If his night-time sleep was regulated it would help him to have regular nap times. Zane's parents established a winding down bedtime routine (see pages 30–31) and decided on regular bed and wake-up times, based on the average amount of sleep he needed for his age (see pages 14–15).

They implemented a gradual retreat plan to teach him how to settle to sleep independently at bedtime and when he woke naturally during the night. They decided to keep one night feed, which they aimed to be after midnight. Additionally, two daytime naps were planned and three regular mealtimes.

Results

On the first morning Zane's parents woke him at the set time. When he had been awake for about three hours he was taken for a midmorning walk so he could sleep; the same pattern was repeated for an afternoon nap. The goal was to establish set nap timings first (see pages 32–35). Once these were in place, the next stage was to settle Zane in his cot for his morning nap.

At bedtime his parents gave him a calm five-minute bath and started their gradual retreat plan to settle him to sleep (see pages 72–74). The first goal was to cuddle and walk with him, rather than rock him to sleep. As expected, it took about 40 minutes for Zane to go to sleep on the first night as he was adapting to the new way of going to sleep. Over the next three nights this gradually reduced, and by night four he was asleep in 15 minutes. When he woke at night they repeated the technique used at bedtime to get him back to sleep, and gave him a feed when he woke after midnight. He was able to nap in his buggy. On the fifth night Zane's parents moved to step two of their gradual retreat plan.

After two weeks of the sleep programme, Zane was settling to sleep at 7.30pm. His first night waking gradually moved later and later, to the point where he slept well until his feed at about 1.30am. His parents found the hardest part was getting him back to sleep in the early hours of the morning; if Zane woke at 5.00am this could take 30 minutes or more.

Establishing a regular bedtime routine is the key to a successful sleep programme.

Steps

Step 1 If your baby or young toddler will only settle with rocking or needs your help to get to sleep, has no set bedtime, wake-up time or naps and at times seems overtired and fractious, start by regulating his sleeping and waking times with a routine that works for your family.

Step 2 Time the last nap so that he is tired, but not overtired at bedtime; if your baby is nine months or older aim for him to be awake by 3.00–3.30pm. Introduce a winding-down routine before both his naps and bedtime to prevent him becoming over-stimulated. You may also wish to use a gradual retreat plan (see pages 72–74) to teach him how to fall asleep in his cot.

Step 3 If your child is reluctant to nap, focus on the timing of them first. If needed take him for a walk in the buggy or a drive in the car to regulate the timings. Once nap times are are established, you can apply a sleep-strategy (see pages 72–81) to settle him in his cot. Work on one nap at a time, and if your baby is not asleep within 20 minutes abandon it and try again the next nap time (see pages 32–35).

Suggested guide for a baby of nine to 15 months. Adjust times to suit your baby.

6.30am Wake-up time

9.30–10.15am First nap

1.30–3.00pm Second nap

6.45pm Start bedtime routine

7.15pm Cuddle and kiss goodnight

7.30pm Asleep

Solution 3 My child can only fall asleep at bedtime with certain props (toddler to six year old)

Try this plan if, like Hannah, your child needs your presence to be able to fall asleep.

Background

Hannah was three years old and lived with her mum, a single parent. As a baby she always fell asleep on mum's lap drinking her bottle, then was transfered to her cot. For the last year she had routinely fallen asleep with her bottle on the sofa in front of the TV next to mum, and was then carried to bed.

Hannah not only fell asleep on the sofa but with age she had become more reluctant to settle at all – she preferred to continue playing. As a consequence, her bedtime was becoming later and later. Hannah's mum wanted her to be asleep by 8.00pm but she often did not settle until after 9.30pm. Hannah was tired during the day and her mum said she had dark circles under her eyes. She was also having more tantrums, was easily upset and her appetite had deteriorated.

Quote from mum
'I need help with setting up a bedtime routine and getting Hannah to sleep in her bed. I feel she needs more sleep and our bedtime routine is stressful and not working for either of us.'

Our view

As Hannah was in the living room with her toys and TV on she found it hard to switch off and go to sleep. Because she had learned to fall asleep on the sofa with the TV and mum close by, she associated this with falling asleep. As a result she was not able to settle independently in her bed. As there were very few boundaries at bedtime Hannah also did not really know what was required of her.

Sleep plan

The plan was to establish a set bedtime with a winding-down routine. Mum implemented a gentle gradual-retreat plan (see pages 72–74) to slowly wean Hannah off her sleep props. A small 'sleep' cushion marked the place where mum would sit while Hannah fell asleep; mum explained to Hannah that she would sit on this cushion until she was asleep (see page 74). The plan was supported by rewards from the sleep fairy for going to sleep nicely at bedtime (see page 83).

Results

Hannah's mum described the first night as 'amazing'. Hannah checked her mum a few times, asking if she would stay on the sleep cushion until she was asleep, but after brief reassurance and a reminder of the 'sleep fairy', she was asleep within 15 minutes. Hannah responded well to the new routine, and she found the sleep fairy's reward in the morning. Night two was even better. On night three Hannah sat up a couple of times to check on mum, who responded by saying 'it's sleepy time Hannah'. Thereafter, progress was fairly typical – a good night followed by a not so good one, but by remaining consistent the 'test' nights gradually disappeared.

After week two Hannah had started to lose interest in the sleep fairy, but she was re-motivated with notes and pictures from the fairy. Hannah was much calmer and happier in the day. She was keener to eat her meals and even try out new foods.

By the end of the third week, 'sleep cushion' was in mum's room and Hannah was falling asleep in her own bed. She called out occasionally but was always reassured by a quick call of 'It's sleepy time Hannah'.

A gradual-retreat plan will help your child learn how to fall asleep in her bed, without your presence, in small incremental steps.

Steps

Step 1 If your child is used to falling asleep while drinking milk or on the sofa with you, start by establishing a regular bedtime routine. For example: offer milk in the living room at 7.00pm; bath at 7.15 pm; straight to the bedroom for stories; and a goodnight kiss at 7.45 pm. Keep bedtime relaxing and calm (see Creating a sleep routine, pages 30–31), resist protests calmly but firmly and try to anticipate excuses.

Step 2 Apply a gradual-retreat plan (see pages 72–74). Sit with your child until she is asleep. Initially you may need to be close by (on a 'sleepy cushion' for example), but maintain minimal interaction. Meet any responses from your child with: 'It's sleepy time; I will stay here until you are asleep'. Once she is asleep, it is important to wait an extra ten minutes before leaving to ensure she is in a deep sleep.

If she gets out of bed to check where you are, rather than picking her up, quietly lead her back to her bed, asking her to climb in, then resume your position. You may need to repeat this a few times, until she understands you will do what you said however many times she gets up. If you are using a reward system, you may need to refocus the rewards for staying nicely in her bed at bedtime, while you sit on the sleep cushion nearby.

Step 3 Your child may take a while to go to sleep in the first few days as she adjusts to the change in routine. If you are using a reward system make sure she fully understands what she needs to do to 'earn' it (see Positive reinforcement – rewards, pages 82–83.

Step 4 If your child is over two years of age, daytime naps should be no longer than 60 to 75 minutes and always avoided after 3.00pm.

Solution 4 My child is anxious and upset at bedtime (three to six year old)

Try this plan if, like Liam, your child is anxious, upset and unable to get to sleep at bedtime.

Background

Liam was six years old and had a younger sister. He had never slept well and his parents had tried everything they could think of. They had consulted friends, trawled the internet and spoken to their doctor, but things were not improving. They were not only concerned for Liam but they never managed any time together.

Liam was confident and happy during the daytime, but as bedtime approached he became upset and anxious. He shared a room with his sister, as his parents hoped that her presence would reassure him.

On a typical evening Liam started getting ready for bed at about 7.00–7.15pm. He would have a bath, brush his teeth, listen to a story and then after a kiss and cuddle, say goodnight. A parent would stay with him for five minutes and then leave to carry out some quiet activities nearby.

Liam would then start getting out of bed, saying 'I can't get to sleep', and become progressively more anxious and distressed. After taking him back to bed numerous times, always reassuring him they were close by, one parent would sit outside the bedroom where he could see them, until he was asleep – this could take up to two hours. After three years of this Liam's parents were desperate for help.

Our view

Liam's bedtime difficulties had gone on for so long that, what started as a common settling problem, had developed into a chronic habit – Liam had never learned to go to sleep on his own. With age, as evening approached, his anxieties increased as he anticipated how he would feel at bedtime. He had become very aware that he was unable to fall asleep and he needed his parents' reassuring presence (see also What if... my child is anxious at bedtime, pages 86–87).

Sleep plan

To avoid bringing up the subject of worries or fears just before bed, Liam's parents were advised to set aside some time in the day or early evening to discuss any concerns he might have.

Liam's bedtime routine started with a calm, relaxing bath. He was then taken to his bedroom to dress for bed, and given a back massage to help him unwind. To build Liam's confidence in his ability to go to sleep independently, his parents used a gradual-retreat plan (see pages 72–74) to slowly wean him from needing them to sit by his door. They would introduce a reward system to encourage him (see pages 82–83).

As part of the first step of the plan one parent would sit on a 'sleep cushion' while Liam went to sleep. Liam was asked to place the cushion in its spot before bath; this way he would know where they would be as he went to sleep. The cushion was to be gradually moved further away from the door towards the top of the stairs, and then down the stairs, one at a time, until it was in the living room.

As Liam naturally fell asleep late, his parents also implemented a late sleep phase plan (see pages 78–79). His bedtime was set to coincide with his sleep time, then gradually brought forward as he learned to fall asleep within 15–20 minutes, until a more appropriate bedtime for his age was reached.

Results

Liam made good initial progress, was asleep within 15 minutes of saying 'goodnight' and not coming out to check where his parents were. He responded well to the 'sleep cushion'; by night four it was at the top of the stairs. He liked the reward system and was already much more positive about bedtime and life in general.

Liam's parents adjusted his routine, gradually moving bedtime earlier; by night seven, he was in bed by 8.40pm and asleep by 8.55pm. He was not checking for his parents and they could sit halfway down the stairs. After four weeks he was falling asleep at 8.30pm and his bedtime anxieties had disappeared entirely.

A child can be happy and confident by day and yet express genuine anxieties come bedtime.

Steps

Step 1 Begin by recording a sleep diary (see pages 70–71) for a week to establish what time your child naturally falls asleep. To see how much sleep is appropriate for the age of your child, check the sleep needs chart on page 14.

Allow 30–45 minutes for your bedtime routine and work out your timings around that. If, for example, he usually falls asleep at 9.30pm, start your routine at 8.45pm and say goodnight at 9.15pm. Keep the bedtime routine calm and focused (see Creating a sleep routine, pages 30–31).

If you are implementing a late sleep phase plan (see pages 78–79) to bring sleep time earlier, your child will be staying up later than normal, so play quiet games such as puzzles or do some colouring in, but avoid screens for the hour before sleep. About ten minutes before you start his routine give your child a gentle reminder that it is about to begin.

Once your child has fallen asleep well for at least three nights, you can move his routine earlier by 15 minutes. If he makes good progress move it again every three to four nights, until he is falling asleep at the desired time.

Step 2 Apply a gradual-retreat plan (see pages 72–74) to help your child confidently fall asleep without you. This can be carried out alongside the late sleep phase plan.

Solution 5 My child resists bedtime and keeps getting up

Try this plan if, like Oliver, your child refuses to go to bed and keeps coming downstairs or calling for you at bedtime.

Background

Oliver was three and half years old, had an older brother and they each had their own bedrooms. Oliver attended nursery five mornings a week and no longer had a nap in the day.

Quote from parents *'We feel so helpless. We just don't know how to keep Oliver in his bed and we know 9.00pm is too late for a child of his age to go to sleep.'*

Oliver's sleep problems started when the family moved house and Oliver was given his own room. After the excitement wore off and the reality of sleeping by himself struck him, he started resisting bedtime. Even with the promise of a reward in the morning, Oliver found it difficult to stay in bed.

Although his parents began to get him ready for bed at 6.30pm, Oliver was never asleep before 9.00pm. Once asleep he did not wake in the night, but mum had to rouse him at 7.30am for nursery. At weekends he would naturally sleep until 8.45am.

The bedtime routine involved both boys. They had a bath together for 20 minutes or so, and would then have a little run around. After getting them into their nightclothes mum read two stories in the older brother's room, then took Oliver to his room. Their dad often came home from work towards the end of this bedtime routine and would talk and share in their fun and games.

Oliver's parents were concerned that he was not getting enough sleep – he always fell asleep in the car, even on short journeys. They also felt that he was easily upset and found it hard to sit still unless he was watching a TV programme.

Our view

Oliver's settling problem had been provoked by anxieties over having a room of his own, and was compounded by his lively and stimulating bedtime routine.

He was on the way to developing a late sleep phase. By the time he got to bed he had a second wind and was unable to fall asleep until he was tired again, an hour or so later. His continual coming downstairs and calling out was a result of a combination of being unable to get to sleep in his aroused state and his worries about being on his own.

Sleep plan

Oliver needed to learn to fall asleep within the normal range of 15–20 minutes of saying goodnight to his parents, then sleep to morning, waking naturally 11½ to 12 hours later.

His parents devised an appropriate bedtime routine, with an emphasis on a relaxing, wind-down period leading up to bed. Suppertime marked a clear division between daytime activities and bedtime. Any wild or rough-and-tumble play was to take place before supper, after supper the boys had some special quiet time reading or drawing with mum.

Oliver's parents introduced a reward system based on the 'sleep fairy' (see page 83) to encourage him to stay in his bed at bedtime and settle to sleep without getting up or calling out.

Results

Oliver's parents successfully implemented a more relaxing bedtime routine and both boys seemed a lot calmer as a result. Oliver was no longer coming downstairs or calling out and mum felt that the reward system had helped with this. In the first two days Oliver took more than 20 minutes to go to sleep; his parents could hear him talking or singing to himself. Even so, by the end of the first week, the latest he had fallen asleep was 8.15pm and the following week he was asleep by 8.00pm, a whole hour earlier than before they started the plan.

Help your child be relaxed and calm at bedtime with a quiet warm bath in a dimly lit bathroom.

Steps

Step 1 If your child has a lively evening and takes time to wind down, start his bedtime routine about 45 minutes before the time you want him to be asleep. Keep bathtime brief – about five minutes – and make sure it stays calm if shared by siblings. Shortening bathtime and limiting the number of bath toys will help to relax him in the lead up to bedtime. If you have two or more children, consider separate bathtimes until the routine is working well.

Try not to chat to your child at this time (just use simple instructions) as the goal is to calm and quieten his 'busy' brain ready for sleep.

Explain the importance of a quiet bedtime routine to your partner too (see pages 30–31). Their involvement is important but it must be a calm process.

Take your children straight into their own bedrooms after their bath; the oldest may be encouraged to get his nightclothes on and read a book while he waits for you or your partner to come and read a story. You could set up a reward system to encourage this (see pages 82–83).

Step 2 About 30 minutes after starting the bedtime routine, say goodnight. Briefly remind your child about the reward the sleep fairy will give if he does not call out or get out of bed.

Step 3 If it takes a little while for your child's body clock to reset itself and for him to relearn the ability to settle to sleep quickly, do not despair. If you and your partner stick faithfully to the new routine and be consistent and clear about the bedtime boundaries – with a little more time – you will achieve your goal. You can expect a marked change in your child's expectations and behaviour within two to three weeks.

Solution 6 My child is awake for long periods in the night

Try this sleep solution if, like Sam, your child settles well at bedtime, but is awake for long periods in the night.

Background

Sam was four years old. He settled well at bedtime, however, every night he woke up and would stay awake for about two hours. He was not unhappy when he woke and his parents could hear him singing and talking to himself. Sometimes he would get up and play with his toys or come through to their room, asking for a drink.

Sam's sleep had always been erratic. He settled perfectly well at bedtime, but woke up for long periods every night. Sam never had a problem with bedtime. He had a bath at 6.30pm, then a story and was in bed by 7.30pm. He would go to sleep almost immediately in his own bed, alone.

Sam usually woke around 2am. His parents could hear him from their room. They would wait a few minutes before going in to tell him to get back into bed and to go to sleep. Once he was in bed they would leave the room, but Sam stayed awake talking and singing. They would go back in several times, until out of exhaustion, they just left him to it.

The situation caused a great deal of strain for Sam's parents. His mum had been under pressure at work and both parents were worried about the impact that the long wakeful periods and resulting sleep deprivation was having on Sam.

Quote from mum *'We want to help Sam sleep through the night. He is tired and grumpy in the day but we do not know how to help him get back to sleep.'*

Our view

Although Sam could fall asleep well at bedtime he had difficulties maintaining sleep; being awake for two hours in the night meant he had low sleep efficiency – the percentage of time spent asleep while in bed. It is calculated by dividing the amount of time spent asleep (in minutes) by the total amount of time in bed (in minutes). A normal sleep efficiency is considered to be 85 per cent or higher.

Sleep plan

The aim was to set up a sleep-restriction plan to consolidate Sam's sleep and so increase his sleep efficiency. Once he was sleeping through the night, the next step was to gradually increase his time in bed. This process would be repeated until he was sleeping well for the average amount for his age – 11 to 12 hours (see page 14).

His parents were asked to keep a sleep diary for a week (see pages 70–71) to see how long Sam slept on average each night. This showed that Sam usually slept for around ten of the 12 hours he spent in bed.

To ensure his time in bed was spent asleep, a schedule was set up for Sam to spend ten hours in bed each night. His bedtime was adjusted so he went to sleep at 8.30pm and he was woken ten hours later at 6.30am; regardless of what happened overnight. As we did not want Sam to associate his bed with being awake in the night, we asked his parents to take him to a dimly lit room when he woke up, read him a quiet story for 15 to 20 minutes, then return him to his room to go back to sleep.

When Sam had been sleeping well for a week, his parents were asked to slowly add time to his night, in 15-minute increments. The first step would be to wake him at 6.45am. Over the next few weeks his time in bed would be slowly lengthened by adding 15 minutes to either the start of the night or his wake-up time. The goal was for Sam to sleep from 8.00pm to 7.00am.

Results

On the first night, Sam was tired in the evening but his parents kept him up until his later bedtime with board games, colouring and reading.

He went to sleep well. He did wake that night, but for an hour and a half, rather than two hours. His parents took him to the spare room for a few quiet stories and, when he seemed sleepy again, returned him to bed. That morning they woke him at 6.30am. Sam was tired in the morning, but he went off to nursery happily.

On the second night he went to sleep at 8.00pm and was awake for an hour in the night, and was woken again at 6.30am. Sam's parents continued to limit his time in bed to ten hours for the rest of the week.

By the start of week two Sam was only waking briefly and returning to sleep quickly. By week three he had started sleeping through the night. His parents maintained a ten-hour night for a full week and then started to increase his time in bed by 15 minutes a week.

Eventually Sam's night extended so that he was falling asleep at 7.30pm and waking at 6.45am.

His parents decided to keep to this schedule as it suited them as a family and Sam was thriving on this amount of sleep.

Keep a sleep diary for a week so you can assess your child's sleep pattern.

Steps

Step 1 Establish a good and consistent bedtime routine for your child (see pages 30–31, Creating a sleep routine).

Step 2 Use a sleep diary (see pages 70–71) to estimate how long your child sleeps on average each night.

Step 3 Base any alterations to his sleep schedule on the length of time your child sleeps. For example, if he sleeps for ten hours, a 7.30pm bedtime moves to 8.30pm, and a 7.30am wake-up time moves to 6.3am.

Step 4 When your child has been sleeping through the night for a week, increase his time in bed by 15 minutes a week, either onto bedtime or morning wake-up time, until you reach your goal.

Solution 7 I have to rock my twins to sleep

Try this plan if you have twins experiencing sleep problems at the same time.

Background

Frankie and Ben were ten-month-old twins who had never slept through the night. Their parents were getting up several times during the night to rock the boys back to sleep.

The twins were born four weeks prematurely but were healthy and growing well. Their three-year-old sister was sleeping in the parents' room while they twins slept in their own room in separate cots.

Grandma lived nearby and came to help settle the boys at bedtime. The boys had a 20-minute fun bath together, then were taken into the living room to get dressed for bed and play with their sister. At about 7.30pm the boys were taken to their bedroom and rocked until they fell asleep, usually about 8.00pm. They woke three or four times every night at around 11.00pm, 2.00am and 4.00 am – but not always together – and had to be rocked back to sleep. Their day started around 7.00am and they had a one hour nap in the morning and one and half hours after lunch – on each occasion they had to be rocked to sleep.

Mum was worried that the twins long bedtime routine meant her daughter went to bed very late. She was also concerned the frequent night-waking was having an impact on the health of the family.

Our view

The twin's bedtime routine was too long, not focused around the bedroom and bathroom, and had become very playful. As a result the twins were excited, over-stimulated and did not associate the bedtime routine with sleep. Both boys could only fall sleep if they were rocked.

Sleep plan

Mum and dad's goal was to shorten and refocus the boys' bedtime routine, and to implement a sleep strategy to help them settle themselves to sleep in their own cots.

Around 6.45pm, their parents were to give the boys a five-minute bath, keeping the lights low and giving them only one toy each. After the bath they were to take them straight into their (dimly lit) bedroom, quietly dress them for bed, tell a calm story or sing a trigger lullaby, then settle them to sleep at about 7.15pm. They were then to use the gradual retreat plan (see pages 72–74) to help them settle to sleep in their cots. To help prevent them waking each other at night their parents decided to play a white noise app.

Two daytime naps were scheduled, 45 minutes in the morning and 90 minutes in the afternoon. For naps, the parents decided to only use the gradual retreat when they were making progress at night.

Results

The new routine meant the boys were much calmer at bedtime. The first step was to replace rocking them to sleep with cuddling, swaying and 'shushing' them to sleep; on night one this took 40 minutes. Once they had been asleep for ten minutes they were put in their cots. When they woke in the night they were settled back to sleep the same way. Both boys fell asleep quickly on their first two wake ups, but by about 4.00am both resisted going into their cots, so their tired parents brought them into their bed so everyone could get more sleep. Over the next two nights the boys took less and less time to settle to sleep. They were going back to sleep in their parent's bed in the early hours of the morning.

On night four mum and dad started settling the boys by standing still and patting them to sleep. As was expected for a new step, they took longer to fall asleep. But by nights five and six they were settling well again. After a week the twins night wake-up time had shifted to after midnight, 3.00am then 5.00am.

By week two mum and dad put them in their cots and leant over the side to pat and 'shush' them to sleep. This was a more challenging step and for the following few nights it took longer for Frankie and Ben to fall asleep, but as the week progressed their parents were able to just sit by the cot and pat them.

By the end of week three, the twins were settling with their parents just placing a hand on them and their wake-up times had shifted to 3.00am and 6.00am. They were now coming into their parent's bed just for cuddles and songs in the morning. Over the next couple of weeks mum or dad could settle the boys with just their presence in the bedroom. In incremental steps they sat closer to the door until they were able to say goodnight to the boys and then leave them to happily go to sleep.

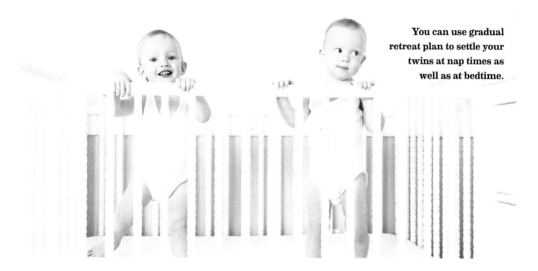

You can use gradual retreat plan to settle your twins at nap times as well as at bedtime.

Steps

Step 1 If you have twins, you may find it easier to set the same bedtime for both, aiming for them to be asleep at the same time. Establish a simple routine that will suit both of them (see pages 30–31),and tuck them in at the same time. Do not worry about one waking the other; most twins do not seem bothered by each other waking, but white noise can help dull out sudden sounds.

Step 2 If either or both your babies need your help to get to sleep, you could try using the gradual retreat plan (see pages 72–74). If they wake at different times apply the technique in exactly the same way as you would for a single child. If both usually wake at the same time you may need another pair of hands to help until they are sleeping better.

Solution 8 My child wakes at night and cannot get back to sleep (toddler to six year olds)

Try this gradual-retreat plan if, like Evie, your child wakes at night and struggles to go back to sleep unless certain factors are present.

Background

Evie was three years old. Her mum was eight months pregnant and her dad worked long hours and often did not get home until after Evie was asleep.

Evie's sleep problems began after a prolonged illness a year earlier when her parents had had to go to her in the night.

Evie's mum would begin to get her ready for bed at 6.45pm and by 7.45pm she would be asleep on her own in her room. However, she would wake crying two to three times most nights.

Each time she woke one of her parents would go to her room, replace her duvet and say 'it's sleep time; it's the middle of the night', lie on her bed until she was asleep, then leave. In the earlier part of the night Evie would go back to sleep quickly, but if she woke after 4.00am she struggled to get back to sleep, so mum or dad would get into bed with her until the morning.

Evie's mum was constantly tired. She had suffered from postnatal depression with Evie and was concerned her lack of sleep during this pregnancy could cause her to become depressed again. Both parents felt irritable and did not know what to do. Evie was also tired in the day, prone to tantrums and didn't eat well.

Summary

Both parents had hoped Evie would return to her usual sleep patterns when she had recovered from her illness, but her night-waking had become habitual. She found the contact with her parents during the night comforting and could now only go back to sleep if one of them was with her.

Sleep plan

The aim was to teach Evie how to return to sleep without the need for her parents. Evie's parents were to start a gradual-retreat plan with a sleep cushion that her parents sat on while she fell asleep (see page 74). To motivate Evie to make the changes, her parents introduced a sleep fairy reward system (see page 83) to encourage her.

Results

Evie woke three times during the first night. Her parents sat on the sleep cushion on her bed instead of lying with her. She did not protest because she was so taken with the idea of a reward from the sleep fairy. She went back to sleep quickly and received her reward from the sleep fairy in the morning.

On nights seven, eight and nine Evie woke twice, but her first wake-up time had shifted later than before. Her parents continued with the plan, and started to move the sleep cushion away from her bed. Progress continued and Evie only protested when the cushion was moved outside her door. Her parents calmly and briefly reassured her that they were there and reminded her of the sleep fairy rules. Three nights later Evie was sleeping through the night.

Over the next three weeks, Evie woke briefly with a murmur and then went back to sleep by herself. Her parents had hardly been disturbed at night. They were very pleased, and the whole family felt much better. Evie was eating better, and everyone reported a much happier and more settled child.

Once you have identified your child's sleep problem, you can take steps to solve it.

Steps

Step 1 If you have been lying with your child when she goes to sleep use a gradual-retreat plan (see pages 72–74), applying each of the steps for a maximum of four nights before moving on to the next. Do not enter into a conversation with your child. Maintain minimum interaction, but use brief statements like 'It is time for sleep; I will sit here with you until you are asleep'. Maintain consistency; do the same thing each time your child wakes.

Step 2 If your child is old enough, you can motivate her with a reward system for going back to sleep nicely (see Positive reinforcements – rewards, pages 82–83).

Step 3 Once she is asleep, always remember to wait ten minutes before leaving her, to be sure that she is in deep sleep.

Step 4 If your child makes a fuss while you are sitting on the sleep cushion, briefly and firmly reassure her you will stay if she is quiet and in bed, and remind her of the reward system. Sometimes you may need to leave the room for just a few seconds if she still does not settle.

Solution 9 My child is frightened of the dark (two to six year old)

Try this sleep plan if, like Ellie, your child is afraid of the dark and worried about monsters in her bedroom or has nightmares.

Background

Ellie was nearly four years old. She was scared to go into her bedroom by herself at bedtime, and was reluctant to go upstairs by herself in the daytime.

Ellie told her mum she was frightened of the dark and thought there were monsters under her bed. In the evening she stayed close to mum and refused to let her out of her sight, even for a moment. After her bath she asked mum to check her room for monsters and insisted on having her bedside and main lights on to go to sleep. Her mum had to promise to stay on the landing while Ellie settled herself. Once Ellie was asleep mum turned off her main light. But in the night Ellie called out to two or three times to check that her parents were nearby, and asking for her light to be put back on.

Ellie's parents were not sure how best to reassure her or how to manage her night-waking without making her more anxious.

Our view

It is very common for children to have fears and nightmares; it is a normal part of their development. But their vivid imaginations and pretend play can mean that scary monsters become real; it is not until they are older that they can tell what is real and what is not. As a result of her fears, Ellie had developed inappropriate sleep-onset associations (see page 53), and needed bright light and her mum close by to be able to get to sleep. When she woke in the night these associations needed to be repeated (see also Sleep disorders and parasomnias, pages 54–57, and What if... my child is anxious at bedtime, page 86).

Sleep plan

Initially the plan was to build Ellie's confidence about being in a room by herself during the day by playing games with her such as hide and seek and treasure hunts. In week two, these games were to be played in the evening with a torch.

Mum checked Ellie's books and the TV programmes she watched to make sure there was nothing to reinforce her fears. She also reassured Ellie that it was normal for her to have fears, but that she was safe and that mum was there to protect her. She discussed them in the daytime, rather than at bedtime and they made 'funny monster' masks to take away the fear factor.

To help Ellie adapt to sleeping in a darker bedroom, a dimmer switch was installed on Ellie's main light. The light was to be gradually dimmed until Ellie was able to sleep with just a small bedside light on all night.

Mum decided to use the 'Excuse me' drill (see page 80) to help Ellie adapt to falling asleep without her. If she woke in the night, mum was to briefly reassure Ellie from the doorway that she was in bed close by.

Results

Over the first two weeks Ellie's confidence to be in a room by herself grew. She really enjoyed playing the games with mum and happily went into other rooms without a thought, even when the room was darkened.

On week three, mum introduced the 'Excuse me' drill at bedtime and Ellie adapted well to the increasingly longer periods of time mum was away. By week four mum was able to say goodnight and go to the living room while Ellie went to sleep and she was only waking once in the night for brief reassurance. Mum no longer needed to check Ellie's room for monsters at bedtime, and in the daytime they enjoyed reading books together and making funny monster masks.

After six weeks Ellie's bedtime fears had disappeared and, while she still thought monsters were real, they were no longer scary for her.

If your child has a fear of the dark or is frightened at night by the thought of scary creatures it is best to discuss her fears in the day, not at bedtime.

Steps

You can use the following steps if your child is afraid of the dark like Ellie, or if she has nightmares and is scared to go to bed.

Step 1 Start by playing games with your child in the daytime to help build her confidence to spend time alone in her bedroom. If she is afraid of the dark, gradually introduce games that take place in a darkened room with a torch.

Avoid discussing monsters, fears or nightmares at bedtime – instead do this in the morning or in the day. You can help take the fear out of monsters by playing silly monster games, creating fun monster masks and even having a monster 'water spray' to keep them away. Never dismiss your child's fears; reassure her that monsters are just pretend and that you are there to keep her safe.

Step 2 Once your child is more confident in the daytime, you can introduce a sleep plan at bedtime, such as gradual retreat (see pages 72–74) or the 'Excuse me' drill (see page 80) to help them to settle without you.

Step 3 If your child insists on having bright lights on at bedtime, slowly fade the lighting level until she can sleep with just a dim bedside lamp. Remember that the conditions at bedtime need to remain the same all night.

Solution 10 My child wakes very early in the morning (toddler to six year old)

Try this early rising sleep plan if, like Lucas, your child is waking very early in the morning and not going back to sleep.

Background

Four-year-old Lucas had always been an early riser. His day usually started at 5.30am, but in the last six months he had been waking at 4.30 or 5.00am and not going back to sleep.

Quote from dad *'I have tried putting Lucas to bed later, in the hope he will wake later in the morning, but it has made things worse as also he wakes more in the night. I really don't know what to do to help him.'*

Lucas had a consistent bedtime routine with his dad that ran very smoothly. Following a 20-minute bath, a couple of stories and a kiss and tuck-in with his favourite bear, Lucas was asleep most nights by 7.30pm. He sometimes woke during the night and called out because he had a bad dream or because his bear had fallen out of the bed, but he was easily settled back to sleep with some brief reassurance.

Recently Lucas's dad had tried moving bedtime to 8.30pm to see if he would wake-up later, but after four weeks Lucas still woke early and was even more tired. Dad found Lucas's 4.30am starts particularly stressful. He was worried how Lucas would cope at nursery as he was having difficulties focusing in class, but also he worked full time and was concerned that the early starts were affecting his own concentration and could put his job at risk.

Lucas would become aggressive, kicking and hitting out at dad in the evening. At weekends, he sometimes fell asleep on the sofa around 5.00pm and he would be in a bad mood when dad woke him.

Our view

There were two main reasons for Lucas' early rising. First, his dad keeping him up later just meant he got less sleep. Sleep deprivation puts the human body into the flight-or-fight mode, triggering an increase in a hormone called cortisol. Normally, levels are low in the evening, and gradually rise towards the morning to help wake us up. High levels right before bed, from being overtired, mean it is hard to fall asleep. Spikes in cortisol in the morning mean early rising is more likely.

Secondly, dad naturally went to bed early and woke early as his sleep rhythm, or chronotype, was that of a lark (see pages 18–19). Lucas, also a lark, needed an earlier bedtime to enable him to have the right amount of sleep each night for his age. This would mean he would fall asleep faster, have better-quality sleep and was more likely to sleep all night.

Sleep plan

Dad was to keep a sleep diary (see pages 70–71) for a week to establish Lucas's natural wake-up time, which was mostly 5.15am. As he needed around 11 hours of sleep for his age, first his bedtime was to be brought forward, so he would sleep by about 6.30pm. His mealtimes were also moved earlier.

Dad and Lucas were to start a bedtime routine with a short bath at 5.45pm, so he was in bed having a story just after 6.00pm and given a cuddle and kiss goodnight at 6.15pm.

Once Lucas had been sleeping for roughly 11 hours, most nights, for two weeks, the plan was to move bedtime later by 15 minutes so the routine would start at 6pm. This pattern was repeated slowly, in 15-minute increments every three to four nights, until Lucas was sleeping from 7.00pm to about 6.00am (see page 77).

A man-made sunrise 'magic' lamp (see page 82) was put in Lucas's bedroom – initially set at 5.00am – to show him when he could get up. A sleep fairy reward (see page 83) was used to motivate him to stay quietly in bed until it came on. Once he was regularly sleeping past 5.00am, the timer could be slowly be moved later in five to 15-minute increments.

Results

Dad was advised to keep filling in the sleep diary to monitor Lucas's progress. For the first two weeks Lucas was asleep very quickly at his earlier bedtime. He woke most mornings at 5.00am; he woke twice at 4.45am. He loved the sleep fairy and was very keen to get his token – he was saving tokens to go swimming with a friend.

He was getting between ten and a half to 11 hours of sleep most nights. He was much happier and calmer in the day. As Lucas was progressing well, in week three bedtime was moved 15 minutes later. He was asleep at 6.45pm, and naturally woke around 5.30am. The magic lamp was reset to come on at 5.30am.

By week five, Lucas was asleep at 7.00pm and he woke between 5.45 and 6.10am. The lamp was reset for 6.00am. Dad was happy with these times and decided to keep a bedtime of 7.00pm.

Steps

Step 1 Fill out a sleep diary for a week to see what time your child naturally wakes in the morning.

Step 2 Work out how much sleep your child needs for his age (see page 14) and what his chronotype is (see pages 18–19). If he is waking early and is a lark, bring bedtime earlier in line with the sleep he needs and his usual waking time.

Step 3 Setting up a man-made sunrise lamp (see page 82) on a timer switch in your child's bedroom will help him know when it is time to get up in the morning. Initially set it to come on at his usual waking time. If he wakes before it is

Encourage your child to wait quietly in bed until the magic lamp comes on to tell him it is time to get up.

on, help motivate him to wait quietly in bed for the light to change with a reward system (see pages 82–83).

Step 4 Once your child has been sleeping well for at least two weeks, start slowly by moving bedtime later by 15-minute increments, until his wake-up time is after 6.00am and he is having the right amount of sleep. Change the morning wake-up lamp in the same way.

Solution 11 My child is sleep-walking

Try this plan if, like Amelia, your child regularly sleep-walks and you are not sure how to manage it, or if you can prevent it happening in the first place.

Background

Amelia was three years and eight months old. For the past few months her parents often found her wandering around outside her bedroom glassy eyed, unaware of their presence and unresponsive, about an hour or two after she had gone to sleep.

Amelia's sleep-walking seemed to coincide with her dropping her daytime nap and recovering from a period of prolonged illness that had affected her sleep. At first her parents had tried to wake her to get her back into bed, but each time they did this she became very upset and took a long time to comfort and settle back to sleep.

Mum and dad were concerned that the sleep-walking might be impacting on her quality of sleep. But they were also concerned about her safety as worryingly Amelia had some sleep-walking episodes after they had gone to bed and they feared what might happen to her when they were asleep.

Both mum and dad remembered sleep-walking as children, so were not surprised Amelia did the same.

Summary

Although scientists do not yet fully understand what causes sleep-walking (see page 54) with both her parents sleep-walking as children, it was not surprising that Amelia had the same sleep disorder. A recent study found that children have three to seven times the risk of inheriting this condition if one or both parents have a history of sleep-walking.

More common in children than adults, it is estimated about 15 per cent of children aged between two and a half and 13 years will have episodes of sleep-walking, and most will grow out of it. As sleep-walking happens in our deepest level of sleep – deep non rapid eye movement (NREM) sleep (see pages 16–17) – one theory as to why it is more prevalent in childhood is due to the fact that children experience more deep NREM sleep than adults.

As well as the inherited element of sleep-walking, having too little sleep or having irregular sleep patterns can increase its likelihood of occurring. In Amelia's case it was possible that her prolonged illness had impacted on her sleep, thereby causing her to have both irregular and disturbed sleep, which contributed to her sleep-walking.

Sleep plan

A plan was put in place to help regulate her body clock and ensure she was having the right amount of sleep. The start of Amelia's bedtime routine was based on her needing about 11 to 12 hours of sleep each night (see page 14). As she woke most mornings at 6.45am her bedtime was based on her being asleep at about 7.30pm.

Her bedtime routine was started at 6.30pm with a short warm bath, then she was taken straight to her dimly-lit bedroom to dress for bed and have one or two stories. Her parents said good night and turned off her light at 7.15 pm. She also had a regular morning wake-up time of 6.45 am.

To keep Amelia safe if she had an episode of sleep-walking, her parents cleared her bedroom floor of toys and books and fitted a stair gate across both her bedroom door and at the top of the stairs.

If they found her sleep-walking, they were advised not to attempt to wake her but to simply guide her back to bed.

To help improve the quality of her sleep Amelia's parents took her for a run around outside or to the park to play every afternoon.

If you, your partner or particularly if both of you experienced sleep-walking as children, be prepared for your child to do it, too.

Results

As she was having more sleep at night Amelia was less tired during the day and her parents reported a reduction in the number of sleep-walking episodes.

With the fitting of the stair gates and clearing of her room, her parents felt reassured Amelia was safe if she did get up in the night.

On the odd occasion she did sleep walk, her parents simply guided her back to bed and tucked her in again.

Steps

Step 1 Fill out a sleep diary (see pages 70–71) for a week to see what time your child sleeps and wakes naturally in the morning.

Step 2 Work out how much sleep your child needs for her age (see page 14) and establish her sleep and waking time around that. Make sure the bedtime routine is calming and unwinding. She may be less likely to sleep walk if she is getting enough sleep.

Step 3 Make sure her sleep area is safe: pick up anything she could trip on and fit stairgates across the stairs and her door so she cannot hurt herself if she wakes when you are asleep.

Step 4 If you find her sleep-walking do not attempt to wake her, just calmly walk her back to bed.

Solution 12 My children share a bedroom and one is waking the other up

Try this plan if one of your children is disturbing the other when she wakes.

Background

Lia was nearly three years old and had been sharing a room with her five-year-old sister Hannah since she was one, but her new night-time waking was disturbing her sister's sleep.

Quote from mum *'We knew what we had to do to help Lia learn to sleep better, but we were concerned we might disrupt Hannah's sleep even more as now she is at school she needs as much sleep as possible'*

Lia's bedtime routine ran smoothly. She and her sister had a bath, then were taken to their bedroom for stories. They usually went to sleep as soon as mum or dad left the room.

Lia had slept well before; the problems started a few months earlier when she moved to a bed. She would come into her parents' bedroom three or four times a night. Each time mum or dad would carry her back, explain that it was not time to get up, tuck her in and leave her to sleep. Eventually, her tired parents would let her into their bed, in the hope of getting some sleep, and to avoid waking Hannah.

After months of disturbed sleep for everyone, and the prospect of Hannah's return to school after the holidays, their parents decided to try to solve the problem. For a week they filled in a sleep diary, which revealed a pattern to Lia's night-waking – her first one was at 10.30pm, then around 2.00am and finally around 5.00am, when she often would not go back to sleep. Hannah slept through Lia's earlier wakings, but she was easily disturbed at 5.00am, which resulted in both of them getting up.

Our view

Lia's night-waking started when she moved to a bed as it gave her a new-found freedom. Her goal was to see her parents and get into bed with them. Because mum and dad were worried about waking their older daughter, they had decided to bring Lia into their bed in the early hours of the morning.

Sleep plan

The plan was to teach Lia to stay in her own bed all night and to give both the girls a point of reference for when it was morning. As the girls shared a room, this required a programme that would cause the least disruption to Hannah's sleep. The preferred approach was to follow a gradual retreat plan (see pages 72–74) and set up a man-made sunrise lamp (see page 82) on a timer with a low-wattage bulb, so the girls knew when it was morning; it was initially set for 5.30am, but if they slept on, the dim light would not wake them. In addition, mum and dad would use scheduled stirring (see pages 80–81), to pre-empt Lia's regular 10.30pm wake-up time.

During the day mum and dad explained clearly to Hannah that they were teaching Lia to be able to go back to sleep in the night by herself. They told her they would be sitting in the bedroom, and introduced a reward system to encourage her to go back to sleep if she heard them. Lia would be rewarded by the sleep fairy if she went back to sleep nicely in her own bed during the night.

Results

Mum and dad took it in turns to stir Lia at 10.30pm. Some nights they just placed a hand lightly on her, other nights they needed to reposition her. They did this every night for a week, then only six the next week. Lia's first wake-up time shifted to 2.00am.

For the other wakings, mum or dad guided her quietly back to bed and sat on the cushion until she went back to sleep. If she requested her parents' bed, she was motivated to get back into bed when reminded of the fairy reward.

Her parents took it in turns to attend to Lia. Worried they may be too tired to hear Lia getting into their bed in the nght, they tied a bell to their bedroom door so they could respond straight away if Lia came into the room.

During the first week Lia woke twice a night and took around half an hour to go back to sleep. She trusted that her parents were going to sit with her while she went back to sleep. and soon she was only waking once a night and returning to sleep quickly. Hannah did not stir and both children were highly motivated by the sleep fairy.

Within two weeks, Lia's parents were able to sit outside the bedroom door. She continued to wake once a night for a few nights, but was easily reassured from a distance.

The timer on the lamp was slowly moved to a later time as the girls became used to staying in bed until the light came on.

Steps

Step 1 Establish a consistent, relaxing bedtime routine lasting no longer than 45 minutes (see pages 30–31, Creating a sleep routine). If your children are old enough, during the day explain clearly the new bedtime 'rules', how the reward system works and what they need to strive for to achieve their rewards.

Step 2 If you have two children sharing a bedroom, to minimize disruption for your other child, choose a technique such as the gradual-retreat plan, which involves responding as soon as your child wakes and staying with them until they return to sleep.

If your child has a well-established bedtime routine and has always settled

Pre-schoolers are more motivated by small, regular rewards.

without you, you do not need to make any changes at bedtime. Continue settling her as before and only use the gradual retreat method for night-waking.

Step 3 If you set up a reward system for the child who has difficulty sleeping, consider a reward system for your 'good' sleeper too. Recognizing positive behaviour will help to reinforce good sleep habits too.

Solution 13 I would like to teach my older baby to fall asleep in his cot

Try this bedtime plan if you would like to start the gentle process of teaching your baby how to fall asleep in his cot for naps and bedtime.

Background

Aidan was six months old and had a three-year-old sister, Grace, who at the same age was diagnosed with reflux and food allergies. Grace had been a fractious, unsettled baby who hardly slept, with the result that mum had very little sleep and suffered with severe postnatal depression.

Even though Aidan did not have the same medical conditions as his sister and was a much more settled baby, mum's nights were still broken and she was worried that she may suffer with depression again. Aiden was currently falling asleep in mum's arms as she breastfed and was then transferred to his cot, so mum wanted to teach him how to fall asleep in his cot at bedtime and for naps.

Aidan's bedtime routine consisted of playtime and a bath with his sister. He was then taken into his parent's bedroom, dressed for bed, read a story and given a feed. By 7.30pm he was deeply asleep so mum transferred him into his cot. He woke two to three times in the night. Each time he had a feed, fell asleep and was transferred back into his cot. If he woke at 5.00am he often stayed awake until his first nap.

Our view

Mum's history of postnatal depression made her feel anxious about Aidan's sleep. She wanted a gentle sleep plan that would teach him new sleep associations without compromising her night-time breastfeeding. Putting Aidan into his cot at bed and nap times while drowsy but still awake, would help prevent sleep-onset associations developing (see page 53).

Sleep plan

The key to making the change was to breastfeed Aidan, then carry out his bedtime routine and put him in his cot while drowsy but still awake.

As Aidan usually fell asleep about 7.30pm, mum decided to offer him his pre-bed feed in a quiet room at 6.45pm. If he became sleepy while feeding mum gently roused him and offered the breast

again. When he no longer wished to feed she gave him a five-minute warm and relaxing bath on his own; his parents would re-introduce a joint bath with Grace once bedtime was working well.

Initially mum was to settle Aidan to sleep rocking and shushing him in her arms using the first step of the gradual retreat plan (see pages 72–74). Dad had offered to do this, but as Aidan was used to mum settling him, she didn't want to introduce too many changes at once. The plan was for dad to settle him from week two. Mum offered Aidan his night-time breastfeeds as usual.

In the daytime mum was to offer him his feeds a short while before his usual nap times.

Results

Week one Aidan took his pre-bath feed well. He did become drowsy, but after mum winded him he fed happily for another few minutes. She then gave him his bath, keeping the lights low. Mum felt the whole routine was much calmer and Aidan seemed more relaxed.

She rocked him to sleep in her arms. As Aidan was more relaxed this took less time than mum had anticipated. He stirred when she put him in his cot so she leaned over and patted and shushed him to sleep. There were evenings when Aidan woke as soon he was put in the cot, but she picked him up, rocked and shushed him to back to sleep. Sometimes she had to do this three or four times. By the end of the week Aidan was settling well and his first waking had naturally shifted later.

As Aidan was not as sleepy in the day, the naps were more of a challenge. Mum gave him 15 minutes quiet time before each nap and played white noise during the nap so that Aidan was less distracted by sounds; both these measures helped him settle more easily.

Week two Aidan developed a cold and so mum decided to pause the sleep plan for a few days until he recovered.

Week three As Aidan was well again dad started to help with the bedtime routine. For the first three nights Aidan took longer to settle, but dad persevered, using the techniques mum had established, and things improved. This meant both parents were able to get Aidan to sleep and mum could alternate between putting either Grace or Aidan to bed.

Start your bedtime routine with a period of quiet time.

Steps

Step 1 So your baby is not overtired and fractious, set a bedtime based on his sleep cues, his naps and when he is naturally sleepy.

Step 2 A consistent bedtime routine with a relaxing bath and a story helps regulate your baby's body clock (see page 77). Your baby will enjoy the familiarity of these regular activites knowing sleep is coming soon.

Step 3 If your baby always falls asleep during his feed, consider offering it to him before his bath so he can begin to learn to fall asleep in his cot.

Step 4 Once your baby is three months old you can consider establishing a gentle routine such as the gradual retreat plan (see page 72–74) to settle him into his cot awake. Babies who are able to fall asleep on their own at bedtime are more likely to do so again when they wake during the night.

Step 5 If your child becomes unwell, pause the plan until he is better. Try to maintain the point you have reached but if this is not possible you may need to restart your plan; illness often affects a child's sleep (see page 85).

Solution 14 My older baby wakes frequently during the night for small feeds

Try this plan if, like Rory, your baby is over nine months old, wakes frequently for small bottles of milk in the night, and is not keen to have either milk or solids during the day.

Background

Rory was nearly a year old, with no siblings. He slept in a cot next to his mum and woke up to six times a night for short feeds. His mum did not mind being woken once a night, but she was due to return to work soon and was increasingly anxious about how she would cope without any sleep.

Rory did not have a set bedtime routine. Generally, he would be prepared for bed at about 6.30pm and would have 200ml (7fl oz) bottle of milk while being cuddled by his mum. He fell asleep in her arms at 7.30pm, when she put him in his cot.

Rory then woke up every night at around 9.30pm, 11.30pm, 1.00am, 3.00am, 4.30am and 5.30am. His mum gave him a feed each time, but he only took about 80ml (2¾fl oz) milk, before falling asleep in her arms, when she put him in his cot. He had a 30-minute nap at 10.00am and another one from 1.30 to 3.00pm in the afternoon; each time he tended to fall asleep on his mum's lap after a bottle of milk.

Because Rory only had small feeds at night mum thought it would be easy to stop them, but when she tried, he had cried so much she was worried the impact this might be having on him. She was also concerned that he was not eating properly in the day, as he was so distracted, so felt she had to give him night feeds to make up for it.

Our view

Rory had learned to suck on his bottle as a way of going to sleep. Consequently, when he stirred into light sleep at night, he struggled to get back to sleep without it. Rather than helping him to sleep, the bottles had become the reason he was waking.

Sleep plan

First, Rory's bedtime routine was restructured. He was given his pre-bed milk before the start of his bedtime routine; mum gave him his last meal earlier to accommodate this. Mum introduced a relaxing and focused bedtime routine and she taught Rory how to settle himself to sleep using a gentle gradual-retreat plan (see pages 72–74).

Finally, a schedule for reducing feeds was set up to wean Rory off his night-time milk. As he only had small feeds, it was decided to slowly shift his first feed time later in 30-minute increments, until he only woke once for a feed (see Spacing frequent night-time feeds for a baby over six months, page 75).

Results

For the first week Rory was offered his usual 200ml (7fl oz) bottle before bathtime, in a quiet room with white noise to help keep him focused. Then after his bath he was offered a small 80ml (2¾fl oz) top-up feed. His mum then followed step one of the gradual retreat plan to rock and shush him to sleep.

On the first night Rory was calm after his bedtime routine and awake after his small bottle, so mum rocked and shushed him to sleep. This took about 30 minutes. The next night he was asleep in 20 minutes with slightly less rocking and shushing, but as expected night three took a little longer.

After four nights mum moved onto step two of the sleep plan – she walked, swayed and shushed him. As it was the start of a new step, it took Rory slightly longer to go to sleep. But over the following two to three weeks he adapted well to the gradual changes. Eventually she could put him in his cot and leave him to happily go off to sleep by himself. In the second week mum also stopped Rory's post-bath bottle.

Mum decided to reduce the number of his night bottles by gradually delaying the first one to any time he woke after 10.00pm. The first four nights, Rory woke just before 10.00pm, so mum comforted him with rocking and cuddles. On the first night he stayed awake until his feed at 10.00pm. The following three nights he went back

to sleep with rocking and woke around midnight and had his first feed then. On night five, mum moved the feed to after 10.30am. She continued to shift the feed by 30 minutes every four nights until Rory woke naturally around 2.00am, when he took a 180ml (6fl oz) feed. Mum then maintained Rory's feed at around 2.00am. If he woke for any subsequent feeds, she offered them as usual. His sleep continued to improve over the next two weeks until he was waking once between 2am and 3am, fed well and slept until morning.

Rory became more interested in his solids and was eager to have breakfast. He had his milk in a beaker during the day.

Steps

Step 1 Choose a bedtime that works for your child and your family, and keep to the same time each night. Establish a relaxing and consistent bedtime routine (see pages 30–31). Giving your child his last feed in the living room (before bath) helps disassociate sleeping from feeding and prevent inappropriate sleep-onset associations (see page 53). You may need to adjust the time of your child's last meal so he can take an earlier bedtime feed. If he falls asleep while having his pre-bath feed, gently sit him up, wind him and when he is awake again offer the rest of the bottle.

With gradual retreat, it is important for your child to be fully asleep before you leave the room.

Step 2 You can help him learn to self-settle using the gentle gradual-retreat plan (see pages 72–74).

Step 3 To decrease the number of night-time feeds your child is having, start slowly by delaying the time of the first feed by 30 minutes. Offer alternative comfort such as cuddles and rocking if he wakes before your goal feed time. Repeat this process every four nights until you reach your goal.

Solution 15 My toddler wakes for breastfeeds at night and I would like him to sleep through

Try this plan if you have decided you would like to reduce or stop night feeds and are not sure how best to do so.

Background

Owen was 19 months old and had a four-year-old sister. Owen has difficulty falling asleep in his cot and woke four to six times each night to feed, which was impacting on the whole family.

Quote from mums *'We need a plan to help Owen fall asleep in his cot and to help him wake less at night. Sleeping through would be amazing, but at this stage we would be happy if he woke once or twice.'*

Owen's mums had tried putting him down awake at bedtime and for his naps but he would become upset very quickly, stand and cry. At night Owen's mums would try settling him by shushing or putting a hand on him. If this failed one of them would pick him up and try to cuddle and rock him to sleep. More often than not none of these methods worked and his mum nursed to sleep.

Lack of sleep meant Owen's mums snapped at each other and neither of them had much energy to play with their four-year-old daughter. Owen was easily frustrated and upset and rather than walking, he preferred to be carried most of the day.

Owen usually had one two-hour nap at about 1.00pm. His usual bedtime routine started at 7.00pm when he was given a bottle of milk while he watched a quiet TV show. He went for a bath at 7.20pm, was dressed for bed and had a story that was followed by a breastfeed, during which he fell asleep, so mum placed him in his cot with his teddy. Both his mums ensured his bedroom was quiet and dark.

Owen was a healthy toddler who was growing well, but he was a fussy eater; he ate a limited range of foods and was reluctant to try anything new.

Summary

Owen currently associated sleep onset with breastfeeding, rocking and cuddling. He was also drinking a large volume of milk during the night; having this many calories at night impacted on his appetite in the day. His frequent night-waking meant the whole family was suffering from sleep deprivation.

Sleep plan

The goal was to teach Owen how to fall asleep at bedtime and nap time independently in his cot. Studies have shown that infants and toddlers who can settle themselves fall asleep faster at bedtime, wake less often at night, and get more than an hour's extra sleep. Owen's parents were keen to follow a gradual retreat plan (see pages 72–74) to wean him off his sleep-onset associations. The first stage would be to offer him his breastfeed earlier in his bedtime routine and cuddle or rock him to sleep instead. His parents decided to breastfeed him instead of giving him a bottle before his bedtime bath. And, as his nap was just after lunch, mum decided to nurse him when he woke from his nap rather than just before it. The plan was to move to step two of the gradual retreat plan once Owen was having one or no night feeds.

To enable Owen to adjust to the reduction in his night-time calories the night feeds were to be reduced by one minute every few nights (see Schedule for reducing night-time feeds, page 76). As he fed on average for roughly 15 minutes, on night one each feed was reduced to 14 minutes. If he fell asleep feeding, mum was put to him put back into his cot, but if he was still awake after the feed, mum would cuddle him back to sleep. She decided to maintain one full feed at around 2.00am or 3.00am.

Results

Week one As Owen was used to a pre-bath bottle, he happily had his breastfeed instead. After bath his mums took it in turns to cuddle and rock him to sleep. He often stirred and sometimes woke and cried when he was put down, so they were advised to wait an extra ten minutes until he was in a deeper level of sleep before putting him in his cot. This helped, and he stayed asleep. His night feeds were slowly reducing and he mostly fell asleep during his feeds.

Week two Owen's night feeds were now only five or six minutes long and he was usually awake at the end, so was cuddled and rocked back to sleep. He continued to wake for his main 2.00am or 3.00am feed.

Week three Other than his 2.00am feed, Owen's parents had weaned him off his night feeds, so began step two of the gradual retreat. Owen was sleeping much more soundly and his first wake-up time was much later – often not until his feed at about 2.00am.

They continued to use the retreat steps to settle him to sleep at bedtime and nap time. It had been hard work, but his parents had been consistent with the programme. Everyone's sleep was much better and Owen's parents had much more energy and time to play.

Steps

Only start this sleep plan when you have decided that this is the right time for you and your child to be weaned off night feeds.

Step 1 Keep a sleep diary for a week so you know when your child usually wakes and how long his average feeds are (see pages 70–71). If you are not already doing so, implement a regular and relaxing bedtime routine (see pages 30–31).

Step 2 Using your average breastfeeding time as a start point, aim to reduce your night feeds slowly by one minute every other night. If you feel you are going too quickly for your child, you can slow down your rate of reduction to one minute every two or even three nights. Once you have reached two minutes you can stop that feed or feeds (see Schedule for reducing night feeds, page 76). Doing it gradually gives your child's body the chance to adjust to having fewer calories at night.

If he is awake after his feed cuddle or rock him to sleep.

Step 3 When you have weaned your child off his night feeds, you may wish to use a gentle sleep plan like gradual retreat to teach him how to settle himself (see Sleep strategies, page 72–81).

Solution 16 My child still wakes for bottles of milk in the night

Try this plan if, like Isla, your young child regularly wakes at night wanting bottles of milk, water or juice.

Background

Isla was 18 months old and still woke up at least three times a night wanting milk. Her mum was 20 weeks pregnant and exhausted by Isla's night waking.

Quote from mum
'I am becoming more exhausted and irritable as my pregnancy progresses. We want Isla to sleep through the night, but we just cannot seem to break the habit of her needing milk.'

Isla had slept well until she was a year old when the whole family went on a long-haul holiday. While they were away they had a very busy time visiting family and friends and Isla was excited and highly engaged by it all. She became very easily distracted during the day and was not interested in her food or milk. Instead she started waking up four or more times a night for bottles of milk.

Isla usually went to sleep in her cot drinking her milk at 7.15pm. During the night she would wake and call out around 10.00pm, 12.00am and again between 4.00am and 5.00am. She usually drank 120–150ml (4–5fl oz) of milk each time and would settle straight back to sleep afterwards.

By day Isla was fussy about her food and had a very small appetite. Mum was worried that she was waking for milk at night as she was hungry, but did not know how to encourage her to eat more in the daytime.

Isla's bedtime routine started at 6.30pm with a bath, sometimes a massage, then a story. Her parents would give her the usual 120ml (4fl oz) bottle of milk, kiss her goodnight, then leave the room. Isla would fall asleep snuggling her blanket and holding her bottle. Isla had one daytime nap in her cot at about 1.30pm and, again, fell asleep after drinking her bottle of milk.

Our view

Isla had become easily distracted at mealtimes, so prefered to take the majority of her milk (and calories) at night. Now the calories she was having at night were impacting on her appetite for food in the day. At the same time, Isla had learned to associate having milk with going to sleep both at bedtime and during the night.

Sleep plan

To change the association between sleep onset and her bottle of milk, Isla was given her milk before her bath so she was always awake afterwards. Her parents were to implement a sleep plan that would help teach her how to fall asleep without the bottle (see Sleep strategies, pages 72–81. At the same time Isla's night-time milk was to be slowly reduced, which would help to increase her appetite in the day.

Results

For the first three nights Isla was a little confused when her milk was offered to her before bathtime and consequently she took less milk than normal.

But mum continued to offer it to her at the same time each evening. By the end of the week Isla happily took her usual 120ml (4fl oz).

The volume of each night-time bottle was reduced by 20ml (³⁄₄fl oz) every other night, starting from 120ml (4fl oz). Isla still woke three times, but was easily settled back to sleep with the reduced amount.

By the end of week two the volume was down to 60ml (2fl oz) and Isla was only waking once. Mum decided she wanted to stop this small bottle now and settle Isla back to sleep with some brief reassurance and back stroking instead. After a few nights of this Isla slept through the night.

At the same time she was offered her pre-nap bottle, about 30 minutes before her usual nap time. Once Isla had adapted to this new time, mum changed the bottle to a beaker.

As Isla was taking fewer calories at night, her daytime appetite increased and she became less fussy with her food.

Aim to decrease the amount of milk you offer your child at night slowly until the feeds have stopped.

Steps

You can follow the steps here to wean your child off night feeds of milk, juice or water.

Step 1 Start your child's bedtime routine by offering her pre-bed milk in the living room before her bath. Any reluctance to this change is usually short lived. Give her a little more time and she will settle into the new routine. You may need to move her last meal slightly earlier to accommodate the change.

Step 2 If you have not already done so aim to establish a regular, relaxing bedtime routine that lasts no more than 45 minutes (see pages 30–31). If the changes make her unsettled at bedtime, sit by her bed and offer brief reassurance by stroking her back or holding her hand. Try to remain consistent and resist

the temptation to give her any more milk at this time (see page 76).

If your child is old enough, you may find setting up a reward system will help motivate her to settle happily with her new routine (see Positive reinforcements – rewards, pages 82–83).

Step 3 You can teach your child new sleep-onset associations using a milk weaning schedule (see Schedule for spacing out feeds, page 75). Reduce the amount

of milk you offer in each bottle by 20ml (³⁄₄fl oz) every other night. If you think your child needs a little more time to adjust to the reduced amount of milk, simply slow down and reduce the amount every three days. When you have reached 30ml (1fl oz) you can stop the feed altogether.

Solution 17 My child wakes very early in the morning

Try this plan if, like Eddie, your child is three years old or more and is waking early, but appears tired and unable to cope with the day.

Background

Eddie was three-and-half years old and, while he was always asleep by 7.30pm, he had recently started waking at 5.00am, when he immediately wanted to get up and play.

Quote from mum *'I am a working single parent and I just cannot cope with the early starts. I do not understand why Eddie wakes so early, especially as he always used to sleep so well'.*

Prior to his early rising Eddie had always slept 11½ hours at night and had had an hour's nap after lunch. Over the last few months his waking time had slowly crept earlier and now he needed an hour's nap every morning at 9.30am. Mum had to wake him from this nap and he would be grumpy for some time afterwards. By late afternoon his behaviour could be difficult, he was easily upset and had frequent tantrums. He struggled to stay awake in the car, even on short journeys. He fell asleep easily at bedtime, getting 10½ hours sleep each night, but he clearly needed more.

Eddie's mum had tried settling him back into his bed when he woke, but Eddie refused to stay quietly in bed. In desperation mum let him get up and watch TV and have some cereal, while she rested on the sofa close by. She found that she had to go to bed early to cope with the early rising. Grandma would come over some weekends to help out, to give mum a lie-in.

Our view

Eddie's mum's sleep diary showed that he had no trouble going to sleep at bedtime and he did not wake at night. However, his early rising meant he was deprived of well over an hour's sleep a night and had built up a large sleep debt, which showed itself in his behaviour.

Eddie no longer needed to nap in the day; having a nap was shortening his night-time sleep. His early morning starts also meant he was inadvertently rewarded for this behaviour, with the TV. Having early morning cereal meant he had also learned to be hungry at 5.00am.

Sleep plan

Eddie's mum was advised that early rising is one of the most difficult sleep problems to solve and changes often take longer to achieve. She kept a sleep diary throughout so she could monitor and see progress.

The aim was to increase Eddie's night-time sleep, so he slept closer to 11½ hours at night, and to reduce, then stop his daytime nap. A simple 'magic' lamp on a timer, or man-made sunrise system (see page 82), could 'show' him when he could get up in the morning. Mum would also introduce a reward system to motivate him (see pages 82–83).

Eddie needed a way of knowing when it was appropriate for him to get up. As he was not old enough to tell the time, he was asked to to stay in bed quietly each morning until the lamp came on, and he would be rewarded for doing so. What Eddie did not know was that the timer would be adjusted slowly over a period of a few weeks, until he was staying in bed until about 7.00am. At the same time his morning nap time was reduced and finally stopped.

Results

This gradual process taught Eddie to stay in his bed and, even if he woke, to drift back to sleep by resting quietly. By making slow and steady progress Eddie's body clock could adjust to having more night-time sleep. Within a matter of weeks he was able to sleep through to an acceptable waking time. The tantrums had almost stopped, he no longer napped in the day or fell asleep in the car and his mum was able to cope better with the demands of working and being a single parent.

Encourage an early riser to stay quietly in his bedroom.

Steps

Step 1 Complete a sleep diary for the week leading up to the start of your programme so you know when your child usually wakes (see pages 70–71). Set up a lamp with a low-wattage bulb and connect it to a timer switch (see page 82). Any small lamp will do as long as your child can see it clearly from his bed but it is not close enough to wake him.

Step 2 On day one, show your child the lamp and explain to him that he should only get out of bed if the lamp is on. Otherwise he should try to go back to sleep or stay quietly in bed. You can use a reward system to encourage your child (see pages 82–83).

For the first week, set it to come on 15 minutes before his usual waking time, for example, at 5.00am if he wakes at 5.15am. This way it will be on when he wakes and he will receive his reward on day one. If he sleeps later, the lamp is not bright enough to wake him.

Step 3 On week two set the lamp to come on 15 minutes later and then move it again a week later. Continue resetting it each week, until you have reached your goal – the waking time that is appropriate for your child's age.

Step 4 It is important for you or your partner to get up when your child wakes and start the day with him as usual. The rest of the day needs to be structured as normal.

Step 5 If you feel your child is napping too much in the day and it is impacting on their night sleep, slowly reduce their nap until their night-time improves.

Solution 18 My child takes a long time to go to sleep at bedtime

Try this plan if, like Aaron, your child sleeps well but at the wrong times, settling very late in the evening, sleeping through the night and waking late in the morning.

Background

Aaron was almost six years old and had an older brother. After being put to bed at night in his own room, he would frequently come downstairs saying he couldn't sleep and wanting extra drinks and snacks, and end up going to sleep very late.

Quote from mum *'We were worried that Aaron was not getting enough sleep and it was impacting on how he coped at school. Bedtime was a stressful time for the whole family'*.

Aaron had sleep problems from birth. He would start getting ready for bed at 8.00pm. One of his parents would go up with him to get his bedroom ready and read him a 15–20 minute story. They would then say goodnight and leave the bedroom.

Aaron would get up numerous times and come to his parents saying he could not sleep. Eventually he would go to sleep alone in his own bed, but not until 11.00 or 12.00pm. His parents had great difficulty waking him at 7.30am and he would be tired and grumpy. At weekends he naturally slept until 9.00am, sometimes 10.00 or 10.30am. He also had night terrors once or twice a week.

Aaron was sleep-deprived, which resulted in him having problems concentrating at school. He argued with his brother and was tearful and easily upset. His parents felt they had tried everything they could think of to settle him earlier but all without success.

Our view

Aaron's parents kept a sleep diary, which indicated that he had a late sleep phase problem. He also had a sleep deficit, which was affecting his mood and ability to concentrate during the day and leading to the night terrors. He needed about 10½ hours sleep each night and was currently only having eight or nine.

Sleep plan

The plan was to use a late sleep phase plan, which was based on Aaron going to bed at the time he naturally fell asleep however late this may be (see pages 78–79). Once he was able to fall asleep within 15–20 minutes of 'lights out', his parents could bring bedtime forward gradually in 15-minute increments, so that Aaron's body clock would have time to adjust to the earlier sleep time. Wake-up time was to be firmly fixed at the same time everyday. This is an important factor in keeping the plan on track. Leaving your child to sleep in at the weekend could cause a shift in his body clock and jeopardize the plan.

As with all sleep programmes it was vital that Aaron's parents ensured he had a relaxing bedtime routine that lasted no more than 30–45 minutes (see page 78).

Results

To begin with Aaron was even more tired because he was woken up at the same time every morning, including weekends. Aaron responded very well to the programme and was falling asleep each night within 15 minutes. After three nights, Aaron's bedtime routine was brought forward by 15 minutes. This pattern was repeated over a few weeks until he was falling asleep well at an earlier time.

After two months, Aaron was asleep most nights by 8.30pm, sometimes 9.00pm, but no later. As he had caught up on his sleep deficit he was no longer having night terrors and he was a much happier boy. School reported he was doing much better and his concentration had improved.

Steps

Step 1 If your child naturally falls asleep too late for his age most nights, you can address the issue by moving his bedtime to when he naturally falls asleep, then shifting his bed and sleep times every three to four days according to the schedule below (see also Resetting your child's body clock, page 77 and late sleep phase plan, pages 78–79).

Step 2 Set a regular wake up time that you can stick to, and wake your child up at that time each day, including weekends.

Step 3 Continue moving the bedtime until your child falls asleep at the desired time. For a child with a deep-rooted late sleep problem, you may have more success if the adjustments are made once a week.

Bedtimes become more enjoyable when your child can fall asleep happily and easily.

Sleeping schedules

Day	Start routine	Lights out	Aim to be asleep by
1–3	10.15pm	10.45pm	11.00pm
4–6	10.00pm	10.30pm	10.45pm
7–9	09.45pm	10.15pm	10.30pm
Next 7 days	09.30pm	10.00pm	10.15pm
Next 7 days	09.15pm	09.45pm	10.00pm *

*Note: You will need to continue this process until your child is asleep at the desired time, based on his wake-up time and his age.

Solution 19　I think my child may be having night terrors

Try this plan if, like Jack, your child shouts out appearing to be frightened, confused and disoriented, usually one to two hours after falling asleep.

Background

Jack was six years old and had a three-year-old sister. He had suffered from sleep problems as a young baby. Now, he had difficulties settling and often woke screaming or shouting not long after going to sleep.

Quote from parents *'We can't understand why Jack's night-time shouting and screaming happens so frequently. It is very upsetting to see him looking so distressed.'*

Jack had boundless energy and seemed to 'survive' on far less sleep than other children of his age – until he was three years old he had woken daily at 5.00am. After Jack's parents moved him into a bunk bed when he turned six he started to sleep-walk and to scream and shout out, always an hour or two after going to sleep. He appeared to be 'locked' into a dream state – not fully awake. So they decided it was best for him not to sleep on the top bunk because it was unsafe.

Jack's sleep-walking or shouting out happened at least three times a week, and more during the school holidays. He resisted bedtime and his parents still struggled to get him to bed before 9.30pm and, in the school holidays, it was even later. But he woke up at 7.15am every day, even at weekends.

Jack's parents were tired and frustrated by his night-time behaviour, especially as they both had stressful jobs. However, he seemed unaffected and was always surprised to hear what he had done the previous night.

Mum and dad tried limiting his intake of sweets and fizzy drinks, but the behaviour continued. They talked to him about any worries or fears, but he appeared to be happy at school and at home.

Our view

As Jack's night-time disturbances happened within two hours of him falling asleep and he was unaware of his actions the next day, it indicated night terrors and sleep-walking (see pages 54–57). He was also not getting enough sleep for his age, and had a long-term sleep debt so was chronically overtired. Sleep-deprived children have a need for more deep sleep (see pages 16–17), and this makes it more likely that a night terror will occur.

Sleep plan

The aim was to ensure Jack had more sleep by getting him to bed earlier. This would be done gradually in 15-minute increments every four to seven nights, so his body clock had time to adjust. The speed at which the time was to be brought forward depended on how quickly Jack fell asleep. As Jack found it difficult to go to sleep, it was imperative that his bedtime routine was focused (lasting no more than 30–45 minutes), relaxing and calm. Jack's night-time disturbances were worse if he was over-stimulated in the day – especially just before bed – so his parents tried to avoid this as well as sugary foods and caffeinated drinks. They also ensured Jack had plenty of outside play in the daytime.

A reward system in the form of a star chart was set up as an incentive for him to relax and lie quietly in his bed at bedtime.

Results

Jack was happy to go along with the new bedtime routine and as the difference in his earlier bedtime was initially very small, he responded well and got his reward. By the end of the first week Jack's parents had managed to get him to sleep 30 minutes earlier. By day eight Jack had stopped having episodes of sleep-walking and night terrors.

From week two onwards, Jack was going to sleep 45 minutes earlier and bedtime was less stressful for the whole family. Jack was still earning stickers or stars for his bedtime behaviour. He seemed happier and his behaviour was calmer. He now had a set bedtime and, just as importantly, a set wake-up time. His parents were advised to maintain these timings to help regulate his body clock and ensure he was getting enough sleep and prevent any reoccurrence of his sleep disturbances.

Steps

Step 1 Introduce a quiet winding-down routine for your child. For example, give him a snack of a banana and warm milk downstairs, then go for a bath and into his bedroom for nightclothes, a story and lights out (see page 31). Make sure he is not having any caffeine or sugar in the evening.

Give your child a quiet, relaxing warm bath as a lead up to bedtime.

Step 2 If your child normally falls asleep very late, use the late sleep phase plan to slowly bring his bedtime forward (see pages 78–79 and Solution 18, page 150–151). But set a consistent wake-up time too. Reward him for going to bed nicely, for example with stars or a sticker chart (see page 83). Explain the reward system to your child, so that he understands what he needs to do to get the stars.

Step 3 Keep a sleep diary (see pages 70–71) to establish the times your child usually sleep-walks or has a night terror. Then, for a week, stir him 15–30 minutes before this time; this has shown to be highly effective in preventing sleep disturbances.

If your child does sleep-walk or have a night terror stay with him, but do not try to wake him or intervene as he will be confused and disorientated and might become upset. Make sure he is safe – you may need to move any objects you think might hurt him.

If your child snores or is waking in the night for any other reason, this may also be the cause of your child's night terrors. Addressing these issues will help stop night terrors.

Depending on the size of your child's sleep deficit and their ability to go to sleep earlier, the programme will probably take two to three weeks to complete.

Solution 20 My child gets out of bed at bedtime and during the night

Try this plan if, like Layla, your child gets up repeatedly after bedtime and repeats this behaviour in the night.

Background

Layla is three years old. She slept well as a baby until she developed an ear infection at the age of two years. After that bedtimes were difficult and Layla kept getting out of bed to seek out her parents in the evening and at night.

Layla had a regular bedtime routine starting at 6.30pm that comprised a bath, nightclothes, milk and a story in her room, teeth brushing, then lights out. At 7.15pm her parents turned off the light, said goodnight and went downstairs. They left her door ajar, with the landing light on. Layla would reappear 15–10 minutes later and she was carried back to bed, kissed goodnight and tucked back in. This would be repeated several times until she eventually fell asleep around 8.30pm. She would also wake a couple of times at night and go into her parents' room. After a cuddle and a sip of water, she would be carried back to bed. She would then wake to start the day at 7.30–8.00am.

Quote from mum *'As a couple we are tired and more prone to arguments. We would like our daughter to go to bed without keep getting up and sleep through the night. But we do not want to use a technique that would upset her.'*

Our view

Layla's sleep disruptions started after a period of illness. Although her parents had maintained a regular bedtime routine, Layla had discovered that getting out of bed meant extra time with mum and dad. They were inadvertently reinforcing her behaviour by cuddling and talking to her each time she got out of her bed, so it had become a habit.

Sleep plan

Her parents started by filling in a sleep diary (see pages 70–71) to assess the time Layla naturally fell asleep. It was important to set Layla's bedtime around her body clock; she may have a 'night owl' chronotype (see pages 18–19) and find it hard to fall asleep early

As Layla was usually asleep closer to 8.30pm her bedtime routine was to start later, at 7.45pm. It was to be calm, quiet and focused around the bathroom and bedroom, and parents were to say good night at 8.15 pm, much closer to her natural sleep time of 8.30pm.

In the daytime they were to explain that she must stay in her bed at bedtime and to motivate her, they would to set up a sleep-fairy reward system (see Positive reinforcements – rewards, pages 82–83).

If Layla got out of bed mum or dad were to calmly and quietly walk her back to her bed, simply saying 'it's sleep time'. They were asked not to cuddle or kiss her or engage in any conversation at this time. After three to four nights, they were to take Layla to her room, but stand roughly 60cm

(2ft) away from her bed and ask her to climb in herself, simply saying 'I will watch you get into bed from here'. Three to four nights later they were to repeat this process but now 'watch' Layla get back into bed from the middle of her room. Over the next two weeks they moved further away from the bed until they were by her bedroom door, then outside the room, on the landing, and so on. If Layla woke at night, her parents were to repeat what they had done at bedtime.

Results

Because Layla's bedtime was now at the time she naturally fell asleep, she was much sleepier when her parents said goodnight. She was excited that the sleep fairy would leave her a reward for staying in her bed. The first few nights went well and she loved her rewards – she even left thank you pictures for the fairy.

On day five she had had a short nap in the car on the way back from nursery, so was not as tired at 8.30pm. Mum and dad decided to move bedtime later as they felt the plan would not work if they started at their usual time. Even so Layla came downstairs soon after her parents said goodnight, but they walked her back to her bed and stood close by as she got back in and then left. This happened twice more and they repeated the process each time, eventually she was asleep by 9.30pm. The sleep fairy did not leave a present the next morning, but instead a note explaining why. Layla was unhappy but said she would try harder that night.

Even though some nights were challenging, her parents remained consistent. The rewards really motivated Layla. And as mum and dad were keeping all interaction minimal, they were no longer reinforcing her 'old' behaviour.

Steps

Step 1 Keep a sleep diary to establish when your child naturally falls asleep. Explain the new bedtime plan to your child and, if you are using a reward system, what she has to achieve to get a reward (see pages 82–83, Positive reinforcement – rewards). Choose a bedtime that is close to her natural sleep time and follow a consistent, relaxing bedtime routine (see page 31). Remind her of the conditions you have agreed when you tuck her up.

Step 2 If your child gets out of bed, guide her back to bed using only simple instructions, without kissing and cuddling her at this time. Calmly and

Illness can trigger a sleep problem.

firmly ask her to get back into bed and tell her you will watch her. Praise her, from your spot, when she does.

Step 3 Start by taking her right up to her bed, then every fourth or fifth night stop a little further away from her bed, until you are 'watching' her get into bed from the

doorway then from out of her room. Repeat this same pattern if she wakes in the night.

Resources

Useful websites

- British Lung Foundation (blf.org.uk)
Up-to-date advice and information on Obstructive Sleep Apnoea

- Eric (eric.org.uk)
Helpful advice and information on bed wetting

- Living with Reflux (livingwithreflux.org)
Provides advice and support for families with children with gastro-oesophageal reflux and reflux disease

- Lullaby Trust (lullabytrust.org.uk)
Raises awareness of SIDS, provides expert advice on safer sleep for babies and offers emotional support for bereaved families

- NHS (www.nhs.co.uk)
Provides general health advice

- ROSPA (rospa.com)
Provides advice and guidance on home safety and use of baby equipment

References

Atun-Einy, O. and Scher, A. (2016). Sleep disruption and motor development: Does pulling-to-stand impacts sleep–wake regulation?. Infant Behavior and Development, 42, pp.36-44.

Bayer, J., Hiscock, H., Hampton, A. and Wake, M. (2007). Sleep problems in young infants and maternal mental and physical health. Journal of Paediatrics and Child Health, 43(1-2), pp.66-73.

Behavioral sleep problems in children: Judith A Owens, MD, MPH: Oct 26, 2019.

Brockmann, P., Diaz, B., Damiani, F. et al. (2016). Impact of television on the quality of sleep in preschool children. Sleep Medicine, 20, pp.140-144.

Dehlink, E., & Tan, H. L. (2016). Update on paediatric obstructive sleep apnoea. Journal of thoracic disease, 8(2), 224–235

Fatima, Y., Doi, S. and Mamun, A. (2015). Longitudinal impact of sleep on overweight and obesity in children and adolescents: a systematic review and bias-adjusted meta-analysis. Obesity Reviews, 16(2), pp.137-149.

Gozal, D., Tan, H. and Kheirandish-Gozal, L. (2013). Obstructive sleep apnea in children: a critical update. Nature and Science of Sleep, p.109.

Gradisar, M., Jackson, K., Spurrier, N. et al. (2016). Behavioral Interventions for Infant Sleep Problems: A Randomized Controlled Trial. PEDIATRICS, 137(6), pp.e20151486-e20151486.

Greer, S., Goldstein, A. and Walker, M. (2013). The impact of sleep deprivation on food desire in the human brain. Nature Communications, 4(1).

Guilleminault, C., Palombini, L., Pelayo, R. and Chervin, R. (2003). Sleepwalking and Sleep Terrors in Prepubertal Children: What Triggers Them?. PEDIATRICS, 111(1), pp.e17-e25.

Havekes, R., Park, A., Tudor, J. et al. (2016). Sleep deprivation causes memory deficits by negatively impacting neuronal connectivity in hippocampal area CA1. eLife, 5.

Haywood, P. and Hill, C. (2012). Rhythmic movement disorder: managing the child who head-bangs to get to sleep. Paediatrics and Child Health, 22(5), pp.207-210.

Hiscock, H., Bayer, J., Gold, L. et al. (2007). Improving infant sleep and maternal mental health: a cluster randomised trial. Archives of Disease in Childhood, 92(11), pp.952-958.

Kim, T., Jeong, J. and Hong, S. (2015). The Impact of Sleep and Circadian Disturbance on Hormones and Metabolism. International Journal of Endocrinology, 2015, pp.1-9.

Martin, J., Hiscock, H., Hardy, P. et al. (2007). Adverse Associations of Infant and Child Sleep Problems and Parent Health: An Australian Population Study. PEDIATRICS, 119(5), pp.947-955.

Mindell, J., Kuhn, B., Daniel, L., Avi, S. and Lisa, M. (2006). Behavioral Treatment of Bedtime Problems and Night Wakings in Infants and Young Children. Sleep, 29, pp.1263-1276.

Mindell, J., Li, A., Sadeh, A., Kwon, R. and Goh, D. (2015). Bedtime Routines for Young Children: A Dose-Dependent Association with Sleep Outcomes. Sleep, 38(5), pp.717-722.

Mindell, J., Telofski, L., Wiegand, B. and Kurtz, E. (2009). A Nightly Bedtime Routine: Impact on

Sleep in Young Children and Maternal Mood. Sleep, 32(5), pp.599-606.

Perrault, A., Bayer, L., Peuvrier, M., et al. (2019). Reducing the use of screen electronic devices in the evening is associated with improved sleep and daytime vigilance in adolescents. Sleep, 42(9).

Pollock, J. (1994). Night-waking at Five Years of Age: Predictors and Prognosis. Journal of Child Psychology and Psychiatry, 35(4), pp.699-708.

Recommended Amount of Sleep for Pediatric Populations. (2016). Pediatrics, 1;38(2), p.e20161601.

Sadeh, A., Lavie, P. and Scher, A. (1994). Sleep and Temperament: Maternal Perceptions of Temperament of Sleep-Disturbed Toddlers. Early Education & Development, 5(4), pp.311-322.

Sadeh, A., Mindell, J. and Rivera, L. (2011). "My child has a sleep problem": A cross-cultural comparison of parental definitions. Sleep Medicine, 12(5), pp.478-482.

Sadeh, A., Tikotzky, L. and Scher, A. (2010). Parenting and infant sleep. Sleep Medicine Reviews, 14(2), pp.89-96.

Stallman, H., Kohler, M., Biggs, S., Lushington, K. and Kennedy, D. (2017). Childhood Sleepwalking and Its Relationship to Daytime and Sleep Related Behaviors. Sleep and Hypnosis - International Journal, pp.61-69.

'The Excuse-Me Drill: A Behavioral Protocol to Promote Independent Sleep Initiation Skills and Reduce Bedtime Problems in Young Children' in Perlis, M., Aloia, M. and Kuhn, B. (2011). Behavioral treatments for sleep disorders. Amsterdam: Academic.

Trajectories and Predictors of Nocturnal Awakenings and Sleep Duration In Infants. (2014). Journal of Developmental & Behavioral Pediatrics, 35(6), p.391.

Picture credits

Index

About the author

Founder of Millpond Children's Sleep Clinic, **Mandy Gurney** (registered nurse, midwife and Health Visitor) has been advising on children's sleep issues for almost 30 years. She was inspired to set up Millpond in 2000 when she became a mother herself and was faced with a baby with allergies and reflux who just didn't sleep. Suddenly having to cope with sleep problems herself highlighted the lack of professional advice and support available for parents. Thus Millpond was born. Since then their success rate in resolving children's sleep problems has been a staggering 97 per cent.

Millpond is now one of the UK's leading authorities on children's sleep, gently guiding and supporting the parents of babies through to pre-teens to help their children sleep better.

Mandy's team of sleep consultants are qualified health professionals skilled in nursing, midwifery and health visiting and have spent decades working in the NHS and Millpond, drawing upon their extensive knowledge, professional experience and expertise to guide parents sensitively through sleep programmes.

Wanting to get the message out about the importance of sleep, Mandy has gone on to set up sleep workshops for health professionals. Since 2007 she has trained thousands of staff within the NHS across the UK and Ireland.

She is frequently asked to write for online parenting sites such as Huff Post, My Baba and Mumfidential, and she is often asked to give expert comment for the national press television, radio and podcasts.

She is the sleep expert and adviser for a number of household brands and companies, including the BBC, Character World, In The Night Garden, Made for Mums, the Gro Company and Essential Parent.

Mandy is the author of *The Bedtime Book* (Ladybird, 2016), a book on sleep in association with the popular children's television programme *In the Night Garden* and two previous editions of *Teach Your Child to Sleep* (Hamlyn, 2005, 2016), which has sold tens of thousands of copies worldwide and been translated into ten different languages.

If you would like to arrange a private consultation to support and guide you through your child's sleep programme email sleep@millpondsleepclinic.com or call 020 8444 4400. For more info visit www.millpondsleepclinic.com

Don't hesitate; every day that goes by is a missed opportunity to get a good night's sleep.

Acknowledgements

Thanks to all the families I have worked with over the years – their personal experiences and positive feedback gave me the motivation to help other parents and write this book.

I would like to also thank my family who inspired me to immerse myself in the world of sleep and to find a passion in helping children and their families sleep well.

Lastly, to pay tribute to the memory of Tracy Marshall, Millpond's co-founder, who sadly passed away. Her work and expertise will live on through Millpond.